Nǐ Hǎo

Chinese Language Course

Advanced Level

by

Shumang Fredlein

ChinaSoft

Nǐ Hǎo 4 – **Chinese Language Course – Advanced Level**
First published 2001

ChinaSoft Pty Ltd   ABN: 61 083 458 459
P.O. Box 845, Toowong, Brisbane, Qld 4066, AUSTRALIA
Telephone (61-7) 3371-7436
Facsimile (61-7) 3371-6711
www.chinasoft.com.au

Written by Shumang Fredlein (林淑满)
Illustrated by Xiaolin Xue (薛晓林)
Software by Paul Fredlein
Edited by Sitong Jan (詹絲桐), Xiaolin Xue (薛晓林)
Typeset by ChinaSoft on Apple Macintosh

Printed in Australia by Merino Lithographics, Brisbane

Companion workbook, audio tapes and CD-ROMs are also available.

ISBN 1 876739 00 2

Preface

Ni Hao 4 is an advanced Chinese language course for senior school students. A different approach is used for this level. There are more opportunities for listening to unrehearsed text and for discussions in Chinese. Topics for this level reflect the diversity of senior students' lives: from school-based interests and activities to personal/social concerns about health, adolescence, part-time work, relationships, customs, technology and environmental issues.

There are four lessons in this level of **Ni Hao**. Each lesson has four sub-topics, followed by example sentences, vocabulary and character lists.

Each sub-topic is divided into five sections: illustrations, text, data box, discussion questions and special item. The *illustrations* section has a series of pictures and a few questions. The pictures reflect the main text and reinforce comprehension. Questions also enhance understanding of the text and are a good testing tool. The *text* section introduces topics and language to be learnt. There are dialogue, articles, letters, diaries and e-mails. Language forms include formal expressions, popular phrases, idioms and colloquial expressions. The *data box* extends the range of expressions from the text. It mainly draws from language previously learnt with minimal new words. Partly colour coded key sentences are in the cartoons. Students substitute the expressions provided for the coloured parts. The *discussion questions* section allows for student focussed conversations. *Special item* includes classical literature, short stories, cartoons and puzzles.

Following the four sub-topics are example sentences, vocabulary and character lists. *Example sentences* demonstrate how a particular word/phrase is used grammatically in a sentence. The *vocabulary list* includes new words and expressions from the lesson. New words and expressions other than those from the main text are printed in colour and need not be memorized. If they appear in a main text later, they are relisted in black. The *character list* includes characters to be learnt, with stroke order illustrated.

All characters learnt from **Ni Hao 1** to **Ni Hao 4** are listed in the last appendix, in number of strokes order. Students can look up the appendix to recap the Pinyin and to check meanings of a particular character.

*   *   *

Finally I would like to thank teachers Peter Chan, Winnie Edwards-Davis, Beth Hart, Chris Kain, Jessy Tu, Ken Wong and Lin Song, who provided helpful suggestions. My gratitude also goes to Sitong and Xiaolin for their dedication, enthusiasm and hard work. And to Jemma and David for their inspiration. Last but not least, thanks to Paul especially for his ongoing support, not to mention doing all software programming. Without him this book would not have been realized.

Shumang, 2001

iv

Contents

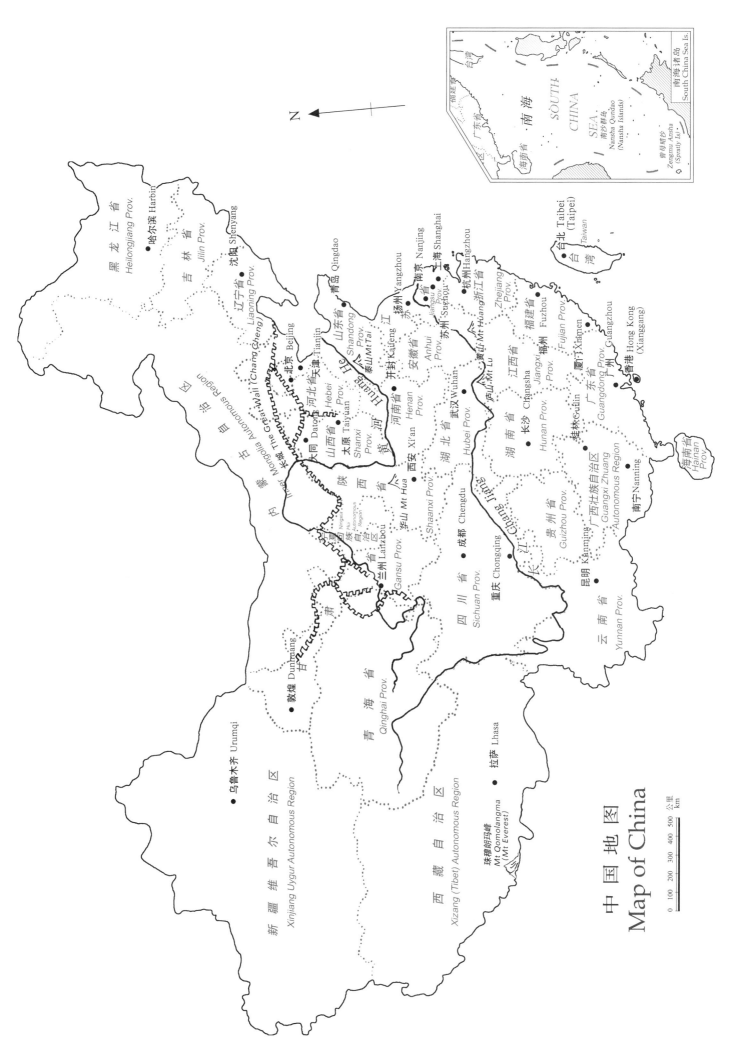

中国地图
Map of China

第一课 又开学了

1 Time Flies （光阴似箭）

Listen and discuss -

1. When do you think this story was told? Give evidence.
2. Where did Lanlan go and what did she do during the holiday?
3. Where did Dawei go during the holiday and how was his trip?
4. What did Xiaoming do and what was the consequence?
5. How did the speaker have her holiday?

（一）光阴似箭
guāng yīn sì jiàn

　　时间过得真快。好象才开始放假，马上又开学了。今天上午到
学校，同学们见了面都在谈自己的假期。

　　兰兰一家人在黄金海岸度了一个星期假。她们天天去海边玩
儿，还去了海洋世界和电影世界。

　　大伟和他爸爸、妈妈去中国旅行了十三天，玩得非常开心，还
交了一个中国朋友。他说有一天，他们在北海公园里迷了路，向一
个学生问路。这个学生很热心，就帮忙带路，最后还送他们回旅
馆。大伟和他很谈得来，就和他交换了住址。回到澳大利亚后，大
伟马上写信向他道谢。现在，他们已经成为好朋友了。

　　小明因为天天在大太阳底下游泳，又没擦防晒霜，全身晒得红
通通的。

　　这个暑假我多半在家陪妈妈。我们一起散步、聊天儿、打网
球。我平常因为忙着学习，没有很多机会和妈妈聊天儿。这次暑
假，我们聊得很痛快。我觉得妈妈很了解我。她不只是我的妈妈，
也是我的朋友。

你暑假都在做什么？

我去海边玩儿。

我在家照顾弟弟、妹妹。

去旅行

去度假

lù yíng
去露营

去海边玩儿

去朋友家玩儿

guàng
和朋友去逛街、看电影

gù
在家照顾弟弟、妹妹

lù
就在家看录像带

就在家看电视

nǎo
就在家玩电脑

你假期过得怎么样？

又刺激，又好玩儿。

忙死了。

yì sī
很有意思

cì jī
又刺激，又好玩儿

yú
非常愉快

不错

sǐ
忙死了

lèi sǐ
累死了

tǐng wú liáo
挺无聊的

读后讨论

1. 你暑假都在做什么？过得怎么样？
2. 你对黄金海岸的印象怎么样？想不想去那儿度假？
3. 如果有人向你问路，你会怎么做？
4. 你有很多谈得来的朋友吗？你们都谈什么？
5. 你游泳的时候，擦防晒霜吗？为什么？
6. 你平常有很多机会和爸爸、妈妈聊天儿吗？你们都聊什么？

都带了

2 The Best Candidate （最佳人选）

jiā xuǎn

Listen and discuss -

1. Who is their form teacher? Give some details of the teacher.
2. Who is likely to become the student leader and why do you think so?
3. What is the person's response to this likelihood?
4. Do you think this person can handle the job and why?

（二）最佳人选

大伟，你知道我们今年的班主任是谁吗？

好象是新来的汉语老师。他姓章。

哪个 Zhāng ？弓长张？

不是弓长张，是立早章。听说他教学很认真，也很关心学生。

你见过他吗？

还没有。等一会儿开班会，我们就会见到他。

对了，同学们都说，今天开班会时要选你当班长。

为什么要选我？我球打得不好，也不会玩乐器。

那有什么关系？大家都说你人缘儿好，学习好，又会玩儿，是班长的最佳人选。

饶了我吧！今年学校的活动那么多：游园会、运动会，还有各种比赛，我怎么忙得过来？

别担心，到时候只要你说一声，我们都会帮忙的。你就放心当班长吧！

放心当班长？班会还没开，谁是班长还不知道呢！

你等一会儿就知道了。走吧，时间快到了，我们进教室去吧！

资 料 箱

中国人怎么介绍他们的姓：

Wáng
王—国王的王
xīng
高—高兴的高
gōng
张—弓长张
Chén ěr dōng
陈—耳东陈
Zhāng lì
章—立早章
Wú
吴—口天吴
mù
李—木子李
Lǚ
吕—双口吕
Lín mù
林—双木林

你觉得他这个人怎么样？

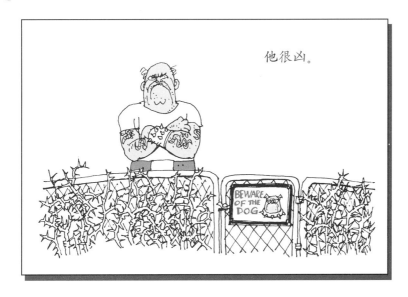

很热心

教学很认真

很关心学生
xiōng
很凶

又会玩儿，学习又好
yuán
人缘儿很好
yuán
没人缘儿

很外向
nèi
很内向

 读后讨论

1. 你们的班主任（zhǔ rèn）是谁？他／她人怎么样？

2. 你们的班长是谁？他／她人怎么样？

3. 你觉得他／她是当班长的最佳（jiā）人选吗？为什么？

4. 你们的班长忙得过来吗？同学们帮他／她的忙吗？

5. 下一次选班长，你要选谁？为什么？

6. 你觉得你自己是个怎么样的人？

❸ Busy as a Bee（忙得不可开交）

Listen and discuss -

1. When are the school extracurricular activities scheduled? What programs are available?
2. What after-school activities do Li Qiu, Xiaoming and Lanlan have at present?
3. What is the speaker busy with after school lately?
4. Do you think the students enjoy their activities? Give support for your answer.

（三）忙得不可开交

每个星期五下午是我们学校的课外活动时间。课外活动的项^{xiàng}目很多。足球、垒球^{lěi}、排球、板球^{bǎn}和体操^{tǐ cāo}是每年都有的，今年又增加^{zēng jiā}了划船^{huá chuán}、空手道^{kōng dào ěr fū}和高尔夫球三个项^{xiàng}目。多了一些选择^{zé}，同学们都很高兴^{xìng}。大部分^{bù fèn}的同学都可以选到自己喜欢的项^{xiàng}目。

除了参加^{chú cān}星期五的课外活动以外，同学们每天下课后也忙着自己的活动。李秋今年加入了交响乐团^{xiǎng tuán}，每个星期有三天要练小提^{liàn tí}琴^{qín}。王小明加入了学校的足球队^{duì}，每个星期要练两次球，又常常要参加比赛。李兰兰下个月要参加全国^{quán}的数学比赛，现在天天都在做练习。

我和班上几个同学正^{zhèng}在忙着筹备^{chóu bèi}今年的游园会。我们班打算摆^{bǎi}一个游戏摊位^{xì tān wèi}，得设计^{děi shè jì}各种^{gè zhǒng}有趣^{qù}的游戏^{xì}，大家忙得不可开交。不过，大家虽然^{suī rán}都很忙，但是^{dàn}忙得挺^{tǐng}开心的。

资 料 箱

● 你参加什么课外活动？

我参加空手道组。

我参加国际象棋组。

Check!

排球队 (duì)

垒球队 (lěi duì)

板球队 (bǎn duì)

乒乓球队 (pīng pāng duì)

班上的篮球队

学校的高尔夫球队 (ěr fū)

划船队 (huá chuán)

体操队 (tǐ cāo)

游泳队

交响乐团 (xiǎng tuán)

合唱团 (hé tuán)

空手道组 (kōng dào zǔ)

太极拳组 (jí quán zǔ)

国际象棋组 (jì qí)

● 今年学校有什么活动？

今年四月，学校要开舞会。

舞会 (wǔ)

晚会

游园会

运动会 (yùn)

音乐会

3 忙得不可开交

读后讨论

1. 你们学校有什么课外活动？你觉得这些项^{xiàng}目有意^{yì}思^{sī}吗？

2. 你觉得学校应该增^{yīng}^{zēng}加哪些活动？为什么？

3. 你参加什么课外活动？是在什么时间？你为什么选这个项^{xiàng}目？

4. 今年你们学校有哪些活动？你参加吗？为什么？

5. 你们学校有足球队^{duì}吗？他们怎么练球？

6. 你们学校的游园会有什么摊^{tān wèi}位？你最喜欢哪个摊^{tān wèi}位？为什么？

很 忙

1
○ 今天下课后我们去逛^{guàng}街好不好？
● 不行，下课后我有小提^{tí qín}琴课。

2
○ 那么，明天行吗？
● 也不行，明天我有钢^{gāng qín}琴课。

3
○ 后天呢？
● 我后天要练空^{kōng dào}手道。

4
○ 这么忙！星期四应^{yīng}该有空^{kōng}了吧？
● 我星期四要练网球，……

5
● ……星期五又有小提^{tí qín}琴课。

6
○ 我看你一整^{zhěng}个星期就只有周末^{zhōu mò}有空了。
● 不，我星期六还要练空^{kōng dào}手道，……

7
● ……星期天有游泳比赛。

4 Always on the net （天天上网）

Listen and discuss -

1. How did Xiaoming and Lanlan get their computers?
2. What does Lanlan use her computer for?
3. What do you think Xiaoming mainly uses his computer for?
4. What's Lanlan's opinion of e-mail?
5. Does Xiaoming's father like the way Xiaoming uses his computer? Why?

（四）天天上网

兰兰，谢谢你昨天发给我的传真，真是帮了我很大的忙。

不用客气。朋友嘛，互相帮忙。咦！那是CD 吗？

这不是激光唱片，是电子游戏光盘。这是我的第六张游戏光盘。

游戏光盘？你买了电脑了？

是去年圣诞节我爸爸送我的。你也有电脑吧？

我有一部，是前年我爸爸送我的生日礼物。它虽然旧了，但是还可以用。不过，我很少玩电子游戏。我通常用它写报告，或上网找资料。你上网络吗？

上，我天天上网。

你都上网做什么？

我发电子邮件给朋友，也和网友聊天。

电子邮件真方便。它比寄信快，比打电话便宜。我也常给台北的大姨发电子邮件。

给我你的电子邮址，改天我发邮件给你。嘿！你也可以进聊天室聊天啊！我觉得挺有意思的。

算了！我妈妈不准我进聊天室，她说那太浪费时间。

真是的！我爸爸最近也不太高兴。他骂我一天到晚坐在电脑前面，不是玩电子游戏，就是上网聊天。

其实电脑的功能很多，你应该多利用。我最近帮数学老师设计了一个网页，大家都说还不错，你看过吗？

没看过。给我网址，我今天晚上可以看看。

资 料 箱

🔵 你用电脑做什么？

我上网买东西。

写作业　　　　玩电子游戏(xì)

写报告(bào gào)　　交网友

学习汉语　　　上网聊天(liáo)

设计网页(shè jì yè)　　上网找资料(zī liào)

发电子邮件　　上网买东西

🔵 你常常上网吗？

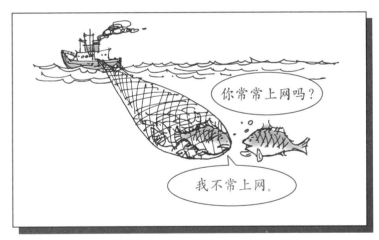

你常常上网吗？

我不常上网。

常常上网

天天上网

一天上三次网

一个星期上两次网

一有空就上网

不常上网

没上过网

不会上网

🔵 你怎么和朋友联系(lián xì)？

你们怎么和朋友联系？

写信、
打电话、
发传真。

Telepathy.

写信(xìn)

打电话

发传真(chuán)

发电子邮件

见面

读后讨论

1. 你有电脑吗？如果（rú guǒ）有，是谁给你的？如果（rú guǒ）没有，打算买一部（bù）吗？

2. 你常玩电子游戏（xì）吗？你觉得好玩吗？你最喜欢哪个游戏（xì）？

3. 你常常上网吗？你上网做什么？

4. 你觉得电子邮件方（fāng）便吗？为什么？

5. 你觉得电脑最好的功（gōng）能是什么？为什么？

6. 你们班有网页（yè）吗？如果（rú guǒ）有，网页（yè）上有什么资料（zī liào）？

去她家

1

✳ 上次和英英吵架（chǎo jià）的事，你向她道歉（dào qiàn）了吗？

✳ 我写了一封信（fēng xìn）给她，可是她没回信。

2

✳ 打个电话给她吧！

✳ 我打过了，可是她不接（jiē）。

3

✳ 发一份传真（fèn chuán）给她，怎么样？

✳ 我们的传真机坏了。

4

✳ 我看发一份电子邮件给她好了。

✳ 我没有她的邮址。……

5

✳ 我看，只好去她家向她道歉（dào qiàn）了。

例 句

1　Time Flies　光 阴 似 箭

才……又……　**just ... again**　It expresses the close occurrence of two events.

好象才开始放假，马上又开学了。

你昨天才迟到，今天又迟到了。

这部自行车昨天才修好，今天又坏了。

见了面　**phrase = v + o**　When a phrase is a combination of a verb and an object, such as

见面, it is common that complements are added between the verb and the object, i.e.

meet	meet three times	met	met three times
见面	见三次面	见了面	见了三次面

other examples:

度假	度一个星期假	度了假	度了一个星期假
写信	写五封信	写了信	写了五封信
交新朋友	交两个新朋友	交了新朋友	交了两个新朋友

向　**towards** or **to**　It indicates the direction or target of an action.

昨天在公园有人向我问路。

他是个好学生，我们都该向他学习。

他帮了很多忙，我们得向他道谢。

着　**v/adj ＋ 着**　"着" is used here to indicate an action in progress, or a continuing state.

考试快到了，大家忙着复习功课。

妈妈在厨房忙着做饭。

他家的门今天一整天都开着。

不只……也……　**not only ... but also**

他不只是个足球迷，也是个篮球迷。

她不只喜欢你，也喜欢我。

2　The Best Candidate　最 佳 人 选

到　**v ＋ 到**　When used after a verb, "到" indicates the outcome of an action.

我昨天见到了新来的汉语老师。

妈妈在叫你，你听到了吗？

小明在电视机上找到了他的鞋子。

例句

当　**to work as, to serve as, to be**

她姐姐想当医生。

我不要当班长。

我请他当我的老师，教我汉语。

听说你当^{gōng}爸爸了，恭喜你！

也　**also**

他教学很认真，也很关心学生。

我球打得不好，也不会玩乐^{qì}器。

她是个网球迷，也是个篮球迷。

过来　(1)　**to come over**

请你过来我这儿。

他为什么不过来？

(2)　忙得过来　"过来" is used here to indicate possibility in managing numerous

things. For impossibility, 忙不过来 is used.

工作这么多，你忙得过来吗？

工作很多，不过我还忙得过来。

工作太多了，我忙不过来。

只要　**so long as, provided, as long as**

只要你说一^{shēng}声，我们都会帮忙的。

只要你用^{gōng}功，一定能学好汉语。

只要冬天一到，她就感冒。

只要你不说，是不会有人知道的。

3　Busy as a Bee　忙 得 不 可 开 交

除了……以外　(1)　**in addition to, besides**　It is often followed by "还" or "也".

我除了喜欢唱歌以外，还喜欢跳^{tiào wǔ}舞。

同学们除了参加课外活动以外，也忙着自己的事。

她每天除了要练钢^{gāng qín}琴以外，也要练小提^{tí qín}琴。

除了我以外，我弟弟也要去。

(2)　**except**　It is often followed by "都".

除了小明以外，大家都来了。

除了你以外，大家都要去看电影。

除了我以外，我们全^{quán}家都要去。

除了下雨天以外，我天天都去游泳。

正在 **in process of** It is used to indicate an action is in progress at the time of speaking or at a specific time. It may be replaced by "在" but carries a stronger emphasis.

妈妈现在正在厨房忙着做饭。

他正在做功课，不要去打扰他。

他正在睡觉，你找他有什么事？

我们正在吃饭，要不要来一起吃？

摆   [bǎi] **to set up, to place, to arrange**

今年的游园会，我们班要摆两个摊位。

晚上有三个人要吃饭，为什么只摆了两双筷子？

他的桌上摆了很多书，可是他都没看。

得   得 can be pronounced in various ways which represent different meanings:

[dé] – **to get, to obtain**

昨天的数学考试，我得了一百分。

这次的足球赛，我们学校得了第一。

他得了流行性感冒，今天不能来上课。

我弟弟得了盲肠炎，医生说要开刀。

[de] – v + 得   used after a verb or an adjective to indicate a degree or a result

他走路走得很快。

他球打得非常好。

我妈妈菜做得很好。

我最近忙得不可开交。

[děi] – **must; need**

考试快到了，我得好好儿用功。

今天家里有事，我得早点儿回家。

快迟到了，我们得走快点儿。

这个周末我不能出去玩儿，因为我得在家照顾弟弟。

虽然……但是……   **although ... yet**

大家虽然都很忙，但是忙得挺开心的。

这部电脑虽然旧了，但是还可以用。

虽然学校有很多活动，但是他什么都没参加。

他虽然加入了足球队，但是不常去练球。

虽然上午天气很好，但是下午下了大雨。

4 Always on the Net 天天上网

发　**to send (fax/e-mail)**

我昨天发了一份传真给北京的朋友。

寄信太慢了，你发传真给他吧！

我常发电子邮件给朋友。

互相　[hùxiāng] **each other, mutually**

他们是好朋友，常常互相帮忙。

我们俩很谈得来，就互相交换了住址。

你们俩应该互相学习。

浪费　[làngfèi] **waste; wasteful**

我觉得上网聊天很浪费时间。

你不觉得一整天坐在电视机前面太浪费时间了吗？

他天天玩电子游戏，浪费很多时间。

买这么贵的鞋，太浪费了吧！

我姐姐买了很多衣服都没穿，真浪费。

生 词

1 Time Flies 光 阴 似 箭

开学	kāixué	*v.* school starts 开- to start, to open
光阴似箭	guāngyīn sì jiàn	*idiom* time flies, literally "Time flies like an arrow." 光阴- time; 似- like; 箭- arrow
才	cái	*adv.* just, only just
放假	fàngjià	*v.* have a holiday or vacation, e.g. 放暑假- have summer vacation 放- to put, to let go, to let out
假期	jiàqī	*n.* vacation 假- holiday, vacation; 期- a period of time
海边	hǎibiān	*n.* seashore, seaside, beach 海- sea; 边- side
海洋世界	Hǎiyáng Shìjiè	*n.* Sea World 海洋- seas and oceans; 世界- world
电影世界	Diànyǐng Shìjiè	*n.* Movie World
开心	kāixīn	*v.* feel happy, rejoice 开- to open, to start; 心- heart
交朋友	jiāo péngyou	*v.* make friends 交- to interact, to cross
北海公园	Běihǎi Gōngyuán	*n.* Beihai Park 北- north; 海- sea; 公园- park
向	xiàng	*prep.* towards or to; *v.* turn towards
问路	wènlù	*v.* ask for directions 问- to ask; 路- road, way
热心	rèxīn	*adj.* enthusiastic 热- hot; 心- heart
带路	dàilù	*v.* lead the way 带- to lead, to bring
旅馆	lǚguǎn	*n.* hotel 旅- to travel; 馆- house, hall

谈得来	tán de lái	*v.* get along well, and usually have a good time chatting 谈- to talk, to chat
交换	jiāohuàn	*v.* exchange, swap 交- to interact; 换- to exchange
道谢	dàoxiè	*v.* express one's gratitude, thank 道- *v.* say, *n.* road, way
成为	chéngwéi	*v.* become 成- to become; 为- to become, to be
太阳	tàiyáng	*n.* sun 大太阳- hot sun
底下	dǐxia	*prep.* under, beneath
擦	cā	*v.* apply, rub, put on
防晒霜	fángshàishuāng	*n.* sunscreen 防- to avoid; 晒- to expose to sunlight; 霜- cream
全身	quánshēn	*n.* entire body 全- entire, whole; 身- body
晒	shài	*v.* expose to sunlight
红通通	hóngtōngtōng	*adj.* red through and through 通- through
多半	duōbàn	*adv.* mostly
散步	sànbù	*v.* take a walk 散- to give out; 步- step
聊天儿	liáotiānr	*v.* chat 聊- to chat, to talk about; 天- sky
着	zhe	*part.* used to indicate a continuing state, or an action in progress
聊	liáo	*v.* chat
痛快	tòngkuài	*adj.* delighted 痛- ache, pain; 快- happy, fast *adv.* joyfully, greatly satisfied
了解	liǎojiě	*v.* understand; *n.* understanding
资料	zīliào	*n.* data, information
箱	xiāng	*n.* box
露营	lùyíng	*v.* camp; *n.* camping 露- to show; 营- camp
照顾	zhàogù	*v.* take care of, look after 照- to take care of; 顾- to attend to
讨论	tǎolùn	*v.* discuss; *n.* discussion 讨- to ask for; 论- to discuss
太阳镜	tàiyángjìng	*n.* sunglasses 太阳- sun; 镜- looking glass, mirror
例句	lìjù	*n.* example sentence 例- example; 句- sentence
生词	shēngcí	*n.* new word 生- unfamiliar; 词- word, term

2 The Best Candidate 最佳人选

佳	jiā	*adj.* good, fine, beautiful
人选	rénxuǎn	*n.* candidate 选- to choose, choice
班主任	bānzhǔrèn	*n.* form teacher 班- class; 主任- director, head
章	Zhāng	*n.* a surname; [zhāng] chapter
弓	gōng	*n.* bow
立	lì	*v.* stand
认真	rènzhēn	*adj.* conscientious, earnest 认- to recognize 真- real, true
关心	guānxīn	*v.* care about 关- to concern, to close; 心- heart
开	kāi	*v.* (1) hold, operate, e.g. 开班会, 开会, 开车 (2) start, open, e.g. 开学, 开始, 开门
班会	bānhuì	*n.* class meeting 会- meeting
选	xuǎn	*v.* elect, choose
当	dāng	*v.* be, work as, serve as, e.g. 当爸爸, 当班长
班长	bānzhǎng	*n.* class leader 长- [zhǎng] leader, chief, [cháng] long
乐器	yuèqì	*n.* musical instrument 乐- music; 器- instrument

1

关系	guānxì	*n.* relation, relationship 关- to concern; 系- to relate to
人缘儿	rényuánr	*n.* relations with people; popularity 缘- fate
饶	ráo	*v.* have mercy on
活动	huódòng	*n.* activity 活- to live, alive; 动- to move
游园会	yóuyuánhuì	*n.* fete 游- to wander, to swim; 园- garden; 会- *n.* gathering, meeting; *v.* be able to
运动会	yùndònghuì	*n.* sports carnival 运动- sports
过来	guòlái	(1) *v.* come over, e.g. 你过来。 (2) used after a verb: preceded by "得" to indicate possibility; preceded by "不" to indicate impossibility, e.g. 忙得过来- possible to manage 忙不过来- impossible to manage
担心	dānxīn	*v.* worry 担- to shoulder, to bear; 心- heart
说一声	shuō yì shēng	*v.* give a word, say (it) 声- sound, voice
放心	fàngxīn	*v.* stop worrying, be at ease 放- to let go, to put; 心- heart
贵	guì	a respectful form of *your*, used in formal occasions
敝	bì	a humble form of *my* or *our*, used in formal occasions
国王	guówáng	*n.* king 国- country; 王- king
吴	Wú	*n.* a surname
吕	Lǚ	*n.* a surname
木	mù	*n.* tree, wood
外向	wàixiàng	*adj.* extrovert 外- outside; 向- direction, to turn towards
内向	nèixiàng	*adj.* introvert 内- inside
糊涂虫	hútuchóng	*n.* blunderer, bungler 糊涂- confused, stupid; 虫- worm
到底	dàodǐ	*adv.* (in a question) after all, on earth, really 到底 is used to indicate a definite reply is requested, e.g. 你到底姓什么？— What really is your surname?
反正	fǎnzhèng	*adv.* anyway, anyhow, in any case 反- reverse; 正- obverse
恭喜	gōngxǐ	*v.* congratulate; *n.* congratulations 恭- respectful, reverent; 喜- happiness

3 Busy as a Bee 忙 得 不 可 开 交

不可开交	bù kě kāi jiāo	*adv.* awfully, terribly (usually used after "得" as a complement) e.g. 忙得不可开交 - be terribly busy 吵得不可开交 - have an awful row
项目	xiàngmù	*n.* item
垒球	lěiqiú	*n.* softball 垒- a base, a rampart
排球	páiqiú	*n.* volleyball 排- to line up
体操	tǐcāo	*n.* gymnastics 体- body; 操- exercise
增加	zēngjiā	*v.* add, increase 增- to increase; 加- to add
划船	huáchuán	*n.* rowing; *v.* row a boat 划- to row; 船- boat
空手道	kōngshǒudào	*n.* karate 空- empty; 手- hand; 道- method, road
高尔夫球	gāo'ěrfūqiú	*n.* golf [transliteration]
选择	xuǎnzé	*v.* choose; *n.* option, choice 选- to choose; 择- to choose
大部分	dàbùfen	*n.* most 部分- part
除了…以外	chúle...yǐwài	*prep.* besides, apart from, in addition to; except
加入	jiārù	*v.* join in 加- to add; 入- to enter

1

团	tuán	*n.* group, organization
练	liàn	*v.* practise, e.g. 练球- to practise ball; 练小提琴- to practise violin
全国	quánguó	*adj.* national; *n.* entire country 全- entire; 国- nation, country
练习	liànxí	*n.* exercise, practice 练- to practise; 习- to practise
班上	bānshàng	in the class
正在	zhèngzài	*adv.* in process of (indicates an action is in progress)
筹备	chóubèi	*v.* arrange, prepare 筹- to plan; 备- to prepare
摆	bǎi	*v.* set up, arrange, place
摊位	tānwèi	*n.* stand, stall 摊- stall, stand; 位- location
设计	shèjì	*v. & n.* design 设- to establish; 计- to calculate
有趣	yǒuqù	*adj.* interesting, fun 趣- interesting, interest
合唱团	héchàngtuán	*n.* choir 合- to combine; 唱- to sing; 团- group
组	zǔ	*n.* group
国际象棋	guójì xiàngqí	*n.* chess 国际- international; 象棋- Chinese chess

4 Always on the Net　天天上网

上网	shàng wǎng	*v.* get on the internet 上- *v.* to go to; 网- net
发	fā	*v.* send (e.g. e-mail, fax); *n.* [fà] hair
传真	chuánzhēn	*n.* facsimile 传- to transmit; 真- real
互相	hùxiāng	*adv.* mutually, each other
电子游戏	diànzǐ yóuxì	*n.* computer/video game 电子- electronic; 游戏- game
光盘	guāngpán	*n.* CD Rom 光- light, bright; 盘- plate
通常	tōngcháng	*adv.* usually
报告	bàogào	*n.* report 报- to report; 告- to tell
资料	zīliào	*n.* data, information
网络	wǎngluò	*n.* internet 网- net; 络- net, vein
电子邮件	diànzǐ yóujiàn	*n.* e-mail 电子- electronic; 邮- mail; 件- document, a measure word for outfit, luggage, matter, etc.
网友	wǎngyǒu	*n.* internet friend
方便	fāngbiàn	*adj.* convenient 方- method, way; 便- [biàn] convenient, urine or excrement, [pián] cheap
电子邮址	diànzǐ yóuzhǐ	*n.* e-mail address 邮- mail; 址- address
邮件	yóujiàn	*n.* mail 邮- mail; 件- document, a measure word
聊天室	liáotiān shì	*n.* chat room
不准	bùzhǔn	*v.* not allow, forbid
浪费	làngfèi	*v.* waste; *adj.* wasteful 浪- unrestrained, wave; 费- to spend, wasteful
真是的	zhēnshìde	*colloq.* used to remark on something unpleasant
骂	mà	*v.* scold, condemn
一天到晚	yì tiān dào wǎn	*phr.* all day long, from morning till night
功能	gōngnéng	*n.* function 功- merit; 能- ability, be able to
利用	lìyòng	*v.* use, make use of 利- to benefit; 用- to use
网页	wǎngyè	*n.* homepage 页- page
网址	wǎngzhǐ	*n.* website 网- net; 址- address
联系	liánxì	*v.* contact, get in touch with 联- to relate; 系- to relate to
道歉	dàoqiàn	*v.* apologize 道- to say; 歉- apology
传真机	chuánzhēnjī	*n.* fax machine 传- to transmit; 真- real; 机- machine

学写字

才 cái *just*	始 shǐ *to start, to begin*	放 fàng *to put, to let go, to let out*	谈 tán *to talk*	非 fēi *not, wrong*
心 xīn *heart*	交 jiāo *to interact, to cross*	园 yuán *garden*	向 xiàng *towards, to*	成 chéng *to become; to succeed*
平 píng *flat, level, ordinary*	忙 máng *busy*	着 zhe *[grammatical word]*	习 xí *to practise*	选 xuǎn *to choose, to elect; choice*
姓 xìng *family name*	认 rèn *to recognize*	关 guān *to concern; to close*	当 dāng *to be, to serve as*	活 huó *to live, alive*
动 dòng *to move*	候 hòu *time*	加 jiā *to add, to increase*	兴 xìng *pleasure*	除 chú *except, besides*
参 cān *to participate*	练 liàn *to practise*	正 zhèng *just, straight*	虽 suī *although*	然 rán *like that*
但 dàn *but*	发 fā; fà *to send; hair*	脑 nǎo *brain*	邮 yóu *mail*	件 jiàn *[m.w. for mail, clothes...]*

第二课 有朋自远方来

fāng

1 Extremely Polite （客气得不得了）

de   dé liǎo

Listen and discuss -

1. Who is Mr Zhang? Where is he from? How long is he going to stay in Australia?
2. Why did Xiaoming's mother decide to invite Mr Zhang to stay with them?
3. How did Xiaoming help Mr Zhang settle in?
4. How did Xiaoming's parents show their hospitality to the guest?
5. What was Mr Zhang's first impression of Australia? Do you agree with him?

（一）客气得^{de}不得^{dé liǎo}了

　　张老师是上海来的交换^{huàn}老师。他要在澳大利亚住九个月。小明的家很大，房^{fáng}间很多，他妈妈决定^{jué dìng}请张老师住他们家。一方^{fāng}面让家里热闹^{nào}点儿，一方面让小明多练习普通^{pǔ tōng}话。

　　张老师到的那天，小明把^{bǎ}张老师介绍^{jiè shào}给他的父母亲^{fù mǔ qīn}。小明的父母亲一直^{zhí}说："欢迎^{yíng}！欢迎！"张老师也不停^{tíng}地^{de}说："打扰^{rǎo}了！打扰^{rǎo}了！"大家都客气得^{de}不得^{dé liǎo}了。

　　小明帮张老师把行李提^{tí}到他房^{fáng}间去，又带他去厨房^{chú fáng}、厕^{cè}所、浴^{yù}室等转^{zhuàn}了一圈^{quān}，然后带他到客厅^{tīng}坐下，和他爸爸、妈妈聊^{liáo}天儿。他爸爸、妈妈一直对张老师说，他们家一切^{qiè}都很简单^{jiǎn dān}，希望^{xī wàng}张老师住得习惯^{guàn}。张老师也一直说他们太客气了。

　　他们问张老师对澳大利亚的第一印象^{yìn}怎么样。张老师说他对这儿的印^{yìn}象很好。他说从机场^{chǎng}出来，每次经过人行横道^{héng dào}，所有的车都停下来让行人先过。他觉得真不可思议^{sī yì}，因为在中国车是不让人的。他又说，这儿风景优美^{jǐng yōu}，空气新鲜^{xiān}，让人觉得很舒服。

资 料 箱

你对那个地方的印象怎么样？

我对那个地方印象很深。

Concrete Work
Strictly No Entry

A very deep impression

印象很深
印象好极了
印象很好
印象不错
印象还好
印象还可以
印象不太好
印象糟透了
没什么印象
一点儿印象都没有

这儿给你的第一印象是什么？

这儿给你的第一印象是什么？

我的第一印象是这儿车都不让人。

空气新鲜
空气很差
风景优美
车都不让人
车都开得很快
车太多，常常堵车

对远方来的人我们常问他们什么？

是自己一个人来的吗？

是自己一个人来的吗？
是和家人一起来的吗？
是来学习还是来玩儿？
吃的还习惯吧？
住得习惯吗？
想家吗？
对这儿的印象怎么样？
打算在这儿住多久？

读后讨论

1. 你家有过从远方来的客人吗？他来做什么？对这儿的印象(yìn)怎么样？

2. 你去过的地方，哪里给你的印象(yìn shēn)最深？为什么？

3. 你的朋友去你家的时候，你把他／她介绍(jiè shào)给你的父母亲吗?为什么？

4. 你去你朋友家的时候，你和他／她父母亲聊天儿吗？聊些什么？

5. 你走人行横道(héng dào)的时候，车都停下来让你先过吗？

6. 你住的地方空气怎么样？风景(jǐng)怎么样？

《论语(lún)》 孔子(Kǒng)

有朋自远方来

有朋自远方来，不亦乐乎(yì hū)？

（论语 1-1）

Isn't it also a pleasure when friends come from afar?

父母在，不远游

父母在，不远游；游必(bì)有方。

（论语 4-19）

Do not travel far when parents are alive, and travel only where planned.

非礼勿动

非礼勿视，非礼勿听，非礼勿言，非礼勿动。(lǐ wù) (lǐ wù) (yán)

（论语12-1）

See no evil, hear no evil, speak no evil, and do no evil.

2 In Rome Do as Romans Do（入乡随俗）

rù xiāng suí sú

Listen and discuss -

1. Who participated in the conversation?
2. What were the choices for breakfast at the Wangs'?
3. What did the guest choose to have for his breakfast?
4. According to the conversation, what breakfast do Chinese usually have?
5. What does the guest usually have for lunch? How about the hostess?
6. According to the conversation, what do Chinese and Australians have for dinner?

（二）入乡随俗

王太太，早！

张老师早！来吃早餐。您要吃土司、麦片粥，还是咸肉加煎蛋？

我吃土司，我自己来烤。

好的，您自己来……喝咖啡吗，张老师？

我不太习惯喝咖啡，有红茶吗？

有。您加糖和牛奶吗？

我都不加。您别忙，王太太，我自己来泡。

张老师，我知道中国人早餐习惯吃馒头或稀饭。我们没有这些，希望您能够习惯。

没问题，"入乡随俗"嘛！我会慢慢适应的。您平常午餐都吃什么？

我午餐吃得很简单，通常吃三明治、汉堡包或热狗等。您在中国午餐都吃什么？

我也吃得很简单，通常吃面条或炒饭。晚餐就比较丰富，有米饭、鱼、肉和蔬菜。

我们的晚餐也比较丰富，有牛排、烤鸡、还有其他各国的菜。

资 料 箱

● 你早餐都吃什么？喝什么？　我吃土司，喝牛奶。

	中国人	澳大利亚人
早餐	馒头(mán)、稀饭(xī)、小菜、包子、烧饼(shāo)、油条(yóu) （喝）豆浆(dòu jiāng)	土司(tǔ sī)、面包、谷类食物(gǔ lèi shí wù)、麦片粥(mài zhōu)、咸肉(xián)加煎蛋(jiān dàn)、水果(guǒ) （喝）茶、咖啡(kā fēi)、牛奶(nǎi)
午餐	汤面(tāng)、炒饭(chǎo)、炒面(chǎo)、饺子	三明治、汉堡包、热狗、烤肉饼、沙拉(shā lā) （喝）果汁(guǒ zhī)、汽水、可乐、咖啡(kā fēi)
晚餐	米饭、鱼(yú)、肉、蔬菜(shū)、汤(tāng)	牛排、烤鸡(jī)、炖羊肉(dùn yáng)、海鲜(xiān)、意大利面(yì)、比萨饼(sà)、印度咖喱(yìn gā lí)、其他各国的菜(qí gè)

● 这个好吃吗？

好吃

好吃极了(jí)

非常好吃

不怎么好吃

好吃，真香

好吃，酸酸甜甜的(suān tián)

好吃，不过太辣了(là)

不怎么好吃，太咸了(xián)

读后讨论

1. 你早餐通常都吃什么？

2. 你午餐习惯吃什么？

3. 你家的晚餐丰不丰富？你们昨天晚上吃什么？

4. 你吃过哪些中国菜？你最喜欢的是什么？

5. 你最喜欢哪国菜？为什么？

6. 你想你是个"入乡随俗"的人吗？为什么？

路过

......

● 请进，请进，不知道你要来。

○ 路过，进来看看你。

● 喝杯咖啡吗？

○ 不喝！不喝！

● 那么，喝杯茶吗？

○ 不，不用了。

● 喝杯果汁吧？

○ 不，您别忙。

○ ......再见！

......

3　A Hearty Meal （吃得很过瘾）

Listen and discuss -

1. What was the occasion and who attended?
2. When and where did the event take place?
3. List the food and drinks provided.
4. What did everyone do during and after lunch?
5. How was the weather?
6. How was the rubbish disposed of at the end of the event?

（三）吃得很过<ruby>瘾<rt>yǐn</rt></ruby>

　　今天小明的爸爸和妈妈请了学校的几位老师和小明的同学去<ruby>附<rt>fù</rt></ruby>近的公园烤肉。

　　这个公园离他们家很近，不到两公里。中午十二点不到，他们就把东西都<ruby>准备<rt>zhǔn bèi</rt></ruby>好，拿到公园的烤肉<ruby>区<rt>qū</rt></ruby>去了。过了十二点，所有的人也都<ruby>陆续<rt>lù xù</rt></ruby>到了。今天吃的东西很<ruby>丰富<rt>fēng fù</rt></ruby>：有烤香肠、牛排和肉<ruby>串<rt>chuàn</rt></ruby>，还有<ruby>法<rt>fǎ</rt></ruby>国面包、生菜<ruby>沙拉<rt>shā lā</rt></ruby>和<ruby>橘<rt>jú</rt></ruby>子、西<ruby>瓜<rt>guā</rt></ruby>等水<ruby>果<rt>guǒ</rt></ruby>；饮<ruby>料<rt>liào</rt></ruby>方面也很多，有<ruby>果汁<rt>guǒ zhī</rt></ruby>、汽水、可乐和<ruby>啤酒<rt>pí jiǔ</rt></ruby>。大家一边吃一边聊天，都吃得很过<ruby>瘾<rt>yǐn</rt></ruby>，也聊得很开心。吃<ruby>完<rt>wán</rt></ruby>烤肉，有的人去打球，有的人继续聊天。今天天气很好，不冷也不热，是烤肉的好天气。下午三点多，大家向小明的家人道谢以后，都<ruby>陆续<rt>lù xù</rt></ruby>走了。

　　小明帮他爸爸、妈妈<ruby>收拾<rt>shōu shí</rt></ruby>东西。妈妈对他说："小明，你把这<ruby>袋垃圾<rt>dài lā jī</rt></ruby><ruby>丢<rt>diū</rt></ruby>到<ruby>垃圾桶<rt>lā jī tǒng</rt></ruby>里。"张老师也过来帮忙。他问："这些<ruby>空瓶子<rt>kōng píng</rt></ruby>和空<ruby>罐<rt>guàn</rt></ruby>子也<ruby>丢<rt>diū</rt></ruby>到<ruby>垃圾桶<rt>lā jī tǒng</rt></ruby>里吗？""不，<ruby>瓶<rt>píng</rt></ruby>子、<ruby>罐<rt>guàn</rt></ruby>子、<ruby>塑料袋<rt>sù liào dài</rt></ruby>和<ruby>报纸<rt>bào zhǐ</rt></ruby>都是可以回收的<ruby>废品<rt>fèi pǐn</rt></ruby>，<ruby>应<rt>yīng</rt></ruby>该放到回收<ruby>桶<rt>tǒng</rt></ruby>里。"小明的妈妈回<ruby>答<rt>dá</rt></ruby>。

　　东西很快就收拾好了。他们把所有的东西都放到车<ruby>箱<rt>xiāng</rt></ruby>里。大家决定走路回家，东西就让小明的爸爸开车<ruby>载<rt>zài</rt></ruby>回去。

资 料 箱

我们怎么请朋友吃饭？

请他们到家里吃火锅。

到家里吃饭、包饺子或烤肉

到家里吃火锅 (guō)

去公园烤肉或野餐 (yě)

去餐厅吃饭或吃火锅 (tīng) (guō)

去饮茶楼饮茶

去小吃店吃小吃 (diàn)

去咖啡馆吃便餐 (kā fēi guǎn)

烤肉时，他除了吃以外，还做些什么？

他帮忙烤肉。

帮忙烤肉

帮忙收拾东西

去打球

就是聊天儿

就是玩电子游戏 (xì)

就是晒太阳 (shài) (yáng)

哪些废品是可以回收的？ (fèi pǐn)

空瓶子是可以回收的。

空瓶子 (píng)　　报纸 (bào zhǐ)

空罐子 (guàn)　　杂志 (zá zhì)

塑料袋 (sù liào dài)　　纸 (zhǐ)

纸箱 (zhǐ xiāng)

读后讨论

1. 你常烤肉吗？都在哪儿烤肉？

2. 你烤肉的时候都吃什么东西？喝什么饮料（liào）？

3. 你烤肉时，除了吃以外，还做什么？

4. 你喜欢烤肉吗？为什么？

5. 你在家常帮忙收拾东西吗？

6. 哪些废品（fèi pǐn）是可以回收的？你们怎么回收废品（fèi pǐn）？

带个盘子去

1

♂ 今天Mary家的聚餐（jù），你要带什么去？

♀ 今天不用带东西，她说只要带个盘子（pán）去。

2

♂ 带盘子（pán）？她们家没有盘子（pán）吗？

♀ 你真笨（bèn）! 当然是她家里人少，盘子（pán）不够用（gòu）。

3

♂ 那么就多带几个盘子（pán）去吧！

♀ ……

4

♂ 回来了。今天的聚餐（jù）怎么样？

♀ 怎么样？真是不好意思（yì sī）！太丢人（diū）了！

5

♀ …大家都带了一盘（pán）菜去，就我一个人没带。

♂ 你不是说只要带一个盘子去就行了吗？

♀ 是啊，她明明告诉（gào sù）我: "Just bring a plate!"

4 Everything is Fine（一切都很好）

Listen and discuss -

1. What is Mr Zhang's impression of Australian students?
2. Can he get used to the food here? Give evidence.
3. How is he keeping himself fit and what are his reasons for that choice?
4. Where did he visit recently and what did he see?
5. With what animal was his picture taken ? How did he describe it?
6. What holiday is coming up? What are his plans?
7. What did he tell his wife to do?

（四）一切都很好

这是张老师写给他妻子的一封信。

玉红：你好！

　　我来澳大利亚已经快一个月了。这儿一切都很好。在学校，老师们都很帮忙，虽然有几个学生上课爱捣蛋，但是大部分学生学习都很认真。

　　小明的家很舒适，他们一家人也非常热情。只是澳大利亚人肉吃得多，生菜也吃得多，所以吃的方面我还不太习惯。不过，我相信过一阵子就会慢慢适应了。

　　我现在天天做运动。早上打太极拳，傍晚游泳。小明家有温水游泳池，是利用太阳能加温的，并不耗电。虽然最近天气开始转凉了，但是我仍然天天游泳，并不觉得冷。

　　上个星期六我去动物园玩儿，看到了很多澳大利亚特有的动物。我喂了袋鼠，还和考拉照了一张相。据说考拉几乎一生都不喝水，只吃桉树叶。它们一整天不是在吃东西就是在睡觉。考拉是稀有动物，和我们的大熊猫一样都是国际上受保护的动物。

　　春假快到了，我打算利用这个机会到各处走走。悉尼歌剧院是一定要去的，有时间的话，我也想去大堡礁和艾尔岩玩儿。你一个人在家，要好好儿照顾自己。

想你

东星　　五月二十六日

资料箱

● 他上课的表现怎么样？
_{biǎo}

他上课很认真。

很认真　　很专心^{zhuān}　　不用心　　很用功^{gōng}　　爱捣蛋^{dǎo dàn}　　爱讲话^{jiǎng}　　常打瞌睡^{kē shuì}

● 我们应该怎么保护环境？
_{yīng　　　　bǎo hù huán jìng}

我们应该多利用太阳能。

多利用太阳能^{yáng}
多利用废品^{fèi pǐn}
回收废品^{fèi pǐn}
不浪费水^{làng fèi}
不浪费电^{làng fèi}
保护动物^{bǎo hù wù}

● 在澳大利亚你最想去什么地方玩？

我最想去黄金海岸玩。

黄金海岸　　　悉尼^{xī ní}
海洋世界^{yáng shì jiè}　　墨尔本^{mò ěr}
电影世界^{shì jiè}　　布里斯班^{bù sī}
悉尼歌剧院^{xī ní　　yuàn}　　堪培拉^{kān péi lā}
大堡礁^{bǎo jiāo}　　阿德莱德^{ā dé lái dé}
艾尔岩^{ài ěr yán}　　珀斯^{pò sī}

读后讨论

1. 你班上的同学上课时的表现(biǎo)怎么样？

2. 你出去旅行时最不能适应(shì yìng)的是什么？

3. 你平常都做些什么运(yùn)动？

4. 你冬天游泳吗？为什么？

5. 你怎么保护环境(bǎo hù huán jìng)？

6. 你喜欢考拉(lā)吗？为什么？

7. 如果(rú guǒ)有朋友来澳大利亚，你想带他们去哪些地方玩儿？

泡好茶

苏东坡(Sū pō)是宋代(Sòng dài)有名的文(míng wén)学家。有一天，他到一座寺庙(zuò sì miào)去。

老和尚看他穿得不怎么样，就对他不怎么客气，只说："坐"，然后回头对小和尚说(shàng)："茶"。

他们聊了一会儿天以后，老和尚觉得这个人还挺(tǐng)有学问的，就对他客气了些，说："请坐"，然后回头对小和尚说(shàng)："泡茶"。

后来，老和尚知道他就是鼎鼎大名的苏东(dǐng míng Sū)坡(pō)，就非常客气

地说："请上坐"，然后回头对小和尚说："泡好茶"。

苏东坡(Sū pō)要走时，老和尚请他留(liú)几个字。苏东坡(Sū pō)就写了一副对联(fù lián)给他：

　　坐，请坐，请上坐；

　　茶，泡茶，泡好茶。

例 句

1 **Extremely Polite** *客 气 得 不 得 了*

决定 **to decide**

爸爸决定买一部(bù)电脑给我。

我们决定今天去看电影。

我决定从明天起好好儿用功(gōng)。

妈妈还没决定假期去哪儿玩。

一方面……一方面……

(1) **for one thing..., for another...**

他去法(fǎ)国一方面是去旅行，一方面是去看朋友。

大家选他当班长一方面是因为他人缘(yuán)儿好，一方面是因为他学习好。

(2) **on one hand..., on the other hand...**

他一方面想考试考得好，一方面又爱玩儿。

她一方面喜欢吃，一方面又怕(pà)胖。

让 **to let; to allow**

妈妈决定让我暑假去中国旅行。

今天地理老师让我们上网找资料(zī liào)。

在人行横道(héng dào)上，车得让行人先过。

昨天妈妈不让我看电视。

把 把 literally means "hold", but does not carry a specific meaning here. It is used in a sentence to introduce an object ahead of a verb to emphasize how it is dealt with, i.e.,

S + V + O	S + 把 O + V
小明介绍(jiè shào)张老师给他的父母亲。	小明把张老师介绍给他的父母亲。
我提(tí)行李到他的房(fáng)间去。	我把行李提到他的房间去。
请你打开窗户(chuānghù)。	请你把窗户打开。
大家拿课本出来。	大家把课本拿出来。
翻(fān)书到第五十九页(yè)。	把书翻到第五十九页。

一直 **(1)** **continuously**

做错事后，他一直说对不起。

今天上数学课时，她一直和同学讲话(jiǎng)。

(2) **straight (in one direction)**

从这条路一直往前走就到我家。

地　　adj + 地 [de]　地 is often used after an adjective/adverb comprising two or more characters to serve as an adverbial phrase, e.g. 不停地, 高兴地.

他不停地向我们道谢。 ^{dào}

她不停地说对不起。

同学们高兴地谈着自己的假期。

不得了　**extremely**　When 不得了 follows "得", i.e., adj +得 +不得了 , it indicates an extreme situation.

他们都客气得不得了。

我三天没吃饭，饿得不得了。

她凶得不得了。 ^{xiōng}

听说爷爷要来，我们都高兴得不得了。 ^{yé}

然后　**then, after that, afterwards**

我们今天打算先去游泳，然后再去看电影。

你明天先到我家，然后我们再一起去看张老师。

一切　[yíqiè] **everything, all**

我们这儿一切都很简单，希望你住得习惯。

家里一切都很好，请放心。

住在他家，我一切都不习惯。

2　In Rome Do as Romans Do　入乡随俗

或　　**or, either...or...**

我午餐多半吃三明治或汉堡包。 ^{zhì bǎo}

我爸爸每天喝四杯或五杯咖啡。 ^{bēi kā fēi}

他通常上网聊天或发电子邮件。 ^{tōng}

通常　[tōngcháng] **usually**

他早餐通常吃土司。

我通常很早起床。

我妹妹通常坐公共汽车上学。

你通常几点回家？

3　A Hearty Meal　吃得很过瘾

准备　**to prepare**

你把东西准备好，我们马上就走。

今天的运动会，我们准备了很多饮料。 ^{liào}

明天要考试了，我功课还没准备好。 ^{gōng}

有的……有的…… **some... while some...**

　　有的人喜欢打球，有的人喜欢游泳。

　　有的人去看电影，有的人去看画展。
　　　　　　　　　huà zhǎn

　　那些苹果有的很甜，有的很酸。
　　　píng　　　tián　　　suān

一边（儿）……一边（儿）…… **do one thing while doing another**

　　他们一边吃饭一边看电视。

　　大家一边喝茶一边聊天。

　　弟弟最喜欢一边玩电脑一边听音乐。

　　咱们一边儿走一边儿聊吧！
　　zán

4 Everything is Fine　一切都很好

2

捣蛋 [dǎodàn] **to make trouble**

　　他上课爱捣蛋，所有的老师都不喜欢他。

　　他们班有很多爱捣蛋的学生，学校的老师都不喜欢上他们班的课。

　　他虽然有时候爱捣蛋，但是人缘儿却很好。
　　　　　　　　　　　　　　　yuán　que

过一阵子　**after a while**

　　我相信过一阵子你就会适应这儿的生活了。
　　　　zhèn　　　　　shì yìng

　　她最近心情不好，希望过一阵子会好些。
　　　qíng　　　　　　zhèn

　　现在我没钱买车，过一阵子再说吧！
　　　　　　　　　zhèn

并不　**not at all**　并 followed by a negative word (不/没) is used to emphasize that the
outcome of a situation is not as it seems.

　　她家的温水游泳池，是利用太阳能加温的，并不耗电。
　　　　wēn　　　chí　　　　　　yáng　　wēn　　bìng hào

　　我今天虽然走了很远的路，可是并不觉得累。
　　　　　　　　　　　　　　　　bìng　　lèi

　　很多人都说数学很难，可是她觉得数学并不难。
　　　　　　　　nán　　　　　　　　bìng　nán

几乎　[jīhū]　(1) 几乎 **almost**

　　　　他几乎每天都很晚才回家。

　　　　她几乎和她妈妈一样高了。

　　　　下午三点不到，几乎所有的人都走了。

　　　　几乎每个去过北京的人都说那儿很漂亮。
　　　　　　　　　　　　　　　　　　piào liàng

　　　　(2) 几乎不/没 **hardly**

　　　　考拉几乎一生都不喝水。

　　　　他今天不舒服，几乎什么东西都没吃。

　　　　她昨天晚上几乎没睡觉。
　　　　　　　　　　　　shuì

　　　　二十年不见，我几乎不认识她了。
　　　　　　　　　　　shí

生 词

1 Extremely Polite　客气得不得了

有朋自远方来	yǒu péng zì yuǎnfāng lái	a friend from afar　朋- friend; 自- from
远方	yuǎnfāng	*n.* distant place　远- far; 方- place
不得了	bùdéliǎo	*adv.* extremely, exceedingly
房间	fángjiān	*n.* room　房- room, house; 间- room, measure word for room
决定	juédìng	*v.* decide　决- to decide; 定- to decide, certain
一方面… 一方面…	yìfāngmiàn... yìfāngmiàn...	*conj.* for one thing..., for another...; on the one hand..., on the other hand..., see p. 41
热闹	rènào	*adj.* bustling with noise and excitement　热- hot; 闹- busy and noisy, to create disturbances
把	bǎ	grammatical word, see p. 41
父母亲	fùmǔqīn	*n.* parents　父亲- father; 母亲- mother
一直	yìzhí	*adv.* continuously; straight (in one direction)
不停地	bù tíng de	*adv.* continuously, frequently　停- to stop
提	tí	*v.* carry (e.g. bucket or luggage)
转圈	zhuànquān	*v.* go around in a circle, turn in circle　转- [zhuàn] go around, [zhuǎn] turn, change; 圈- circle
然后	ránhòu	*adv.* afterwards, then
一切	yíqiè	*n.* everything, all
希望	xīwàng	*v.* hope　希- to hope; 望- to expect
习惯	xíguàn	*v.* get used to　习- to be used to, to practise; 惯- to get used to
经过	jīngguò	*v.* go past　经- to go through; 过- to go across or pass
人行横道	rénxíng héngdào	*n.* pedestrian crossing　人- people; 行- to walk; 横- horizontal; 道- way
不可思议	bù kě sīyì	*adj.* unbelievable, beyond one's imagination　可- to be able to; 思- to think; 议- to discuss
风景	fēngjǐng	*n.* scenery　风- wind; 景- view, scene
优美	yōuměi	*adj.* fine, exquisite　优- excellent, outstanding; 美- beautiful
空气	kōngqì	*n.* air
新鲜	xīnxiān	*adj.* fresh　新- new; 鲜- fresh
差	chà	*adj.* poor, not up to standard; *v.* differ (by), be short
论语	Lúnyǔ	*n.* 'The Analects of Confucius'《论语》is a collection of Confucius' conversations with his disciples. Although the language is in classical Chinese, Confucius' sayings are still often quoted by the Chinese.
孔子	Kǒngzǐ	*n.* Confucius (551 BC – 479 BC), Chinese philosopher and teacher of morals
怕	pà	*v.* be afraid of
翻	fān	*v.* turn over
讲话	jiǎnghuà	*v.* talk, speak　讲- to speak, to talk

2　In Rome Do as Romans Do　入 乡 随 俗

入乡随俗	rù xiāng suí sú	*idiom* when in Rome, do as the Romans do　入- to enter; 乡- country, village; 随- to follow; 俗- custom
土司	tǔsī	*n.* toast [transliteration]

麦片粥	màipiànzhōu	*n.* oatmeal porridge 麦片- oatmeal; 粥- porridge
咸肉	xiánròu	*n.* bacon 咸- salty; 肉- meat
煎蛋	jiāndàn	*n.* fried egg 煎- shallow-fried; 蛋- egg
烤	kǎo	*v.* toast, bake, roast
咖啡	kāfēi	*n.* coffee
红茶	hóngchá	*n.* black tea
加	jiā	*v.* add
糖	táng	*n.* sugar
泡	pào	*v.* brew (tea or coffee), soak
馒头	mántou	*n.* plain steamed bun
稀饭	xīfàn	*n.* rice gruel, porridge 稀- watery, thin (liquids); 饭- rice
能够	nénggòu	*aux.* can, be capable of 能- be able to; 够- enough, adequate
问题	wèntí	*n.* problem, question 问- to ask; 题- question, topic
适应	shìyìng	*v.* adapt, get used to 适- to suit, comfortable; 应- [yìng] to adapt, [yīng] should
等	děng	*pron.* and so on, and so forth; *v.* wait
面条	miàntiáo	*n.* noodles
丰富	fēngfù	*adj.* diverse and plentiful 丰- plentiful, abundant; 富- abundant, wealthy
蔬菜	shūcài	*n.* vegetable 蔬- vegetable; 菜- vegetable
烤鸡	kǎojī	*n.* barbecue chicken 烤- to toast, to bake, to roast; 鸡- chicken
其他	qítā	*pron.* other, others 其- that, such; 他- other, he, him
各国	gèguó	*n.* every country 各- each, every; 国- country, nation
小菜	xiǎocài	*n.* 1. side dish; 2. relishes, pickles, etc.
烧饼	shāobǐng	*n.* baked sesame seed flatcake 烧- to bake, to cook, to burn; 饼- cake, biscuit, cookie
油条	yóutiáo	*n.* deep-fried twisted dough stick 油- oil, oily; 条- strip
豆浆	dòujiāng	*n.* soya milk 豆- bean; 浆- thick fluid
谷类食物	gǔ lèi shíwù	*n.* cereal 谷- grain; 类- kind; 食物- food
汤面	tāngmiàn	*n.* noodle soup 汤- soup; 面- noodle
炒面	chǎomiàn	*n.* fried noodle 炒- stir-fried; 面- noodle
烤肉饼	kǎoròubǐng	*n.* meat pie
沙拉	shālā	*n.* salad [transliteration]
炖羊肉	dùnyángròu	*n.* lamb stew 炖- to stew; 羊肉- lamb
海鲜	hǎixiān	*n.* seafood 海- sea; 鲜- fresh
意大利面	Yìdàlìmiàn	*n.* pasta (spaghetti, lasagne...) 意大利- Italy
比萨饼	bǐsàbǐng	*n.* pizza [transliteration]
印度	Yìndù	*n.* India
咖喱	gālí	*n.* curry [transliteration]
香	xiāng	*adj.* appetizing, fragrant, aromatic
辣	là	*adj.* hot (of taste)
咸	xián	*adj.* salty
路过	lùguò	*v.* pass by 路- road; 过- to pass; to cross

3　A Hearty Meal　吃得很过瘾

烤肉	kǎoròu	*v. & n.* barbecue 烤- to grill, to toast; 肉- meat
区	qū	*n.* area, district
陆续	lùxù	*adv.* one after another 陆- land; 续- to continue

第二课　有朋自远方来

46

生词

香肠	xiāngcháng	*n.* sausage 香- aromatic, fragrant; 肠- intestine
肉串	ròuchuàn	*n.* kebab 肉- meat; 串- a string of
生菜	shēngcài	*n.* lettuce, raw vegetable 生- raw, birth; 菜- vegetable
沙拉	shālā	*n.* salad [transliteration]
啤酒	píjiǔ	*n.* beer
一边……一边……	yìbiān...yìbiān...	do one thing while doing another, e.g. 一边吃饭一边看电视- watch TV while eating
完	wán	*v.* finish; *adj.* complete
有的	yǒude	*adj.* some, a few
继续	jìxù	*v.* continue
以后	yǐhòu	*adv.* after, later, afterwards
垃圾	lājī	*n.* rubbish, garbage
丢	diū	*v.* throw; lose
桶	tǒng	*n.* bin, bucket, barrel
空	kōng	*adj.* empty; [kòng] *n.* free time
瓶子	píngzi	*n.* bottle, jar 瓶- bottle, jar; 子- [zi] suffix for some common nouns with one character, [zǐ] son
罐子	guànzi	*n.* tin, can, jar, jug
塑料袋	sùliàodài	*n.* plastic bag 塑料- plastic; 袋- bag
回收	huíshōu	*v.* recycle 回- to return; 收- to collect
废品	fèipǐn	*n.* junk, waste 废- waste; 品- article
车箱	chēxiāng	*n.* trunk, boot (of car)
载	zài	*v.* convey by vehicles, ships, etc.
火锅	huǒguō	*n.* hot pot 火- fire; 锅- pot, wok
野餐	yěcān	*n.* picnic 野- countryside; 餐- meal
餐厅	cāntīng	*n.* restaurant 餐- meal; 厅- hall
小吃店	xiǎochīdiàn	*n.* small restaurant, snack bar 小吃- snack
咖啡馆	kāfēiguǎn	*n.* coffee shop 咖啡- coffee; 馆- building, shop
便餐	biàncān	*n.* simple meal
纸箱	zhǐxiāng	*n.* carton 纸- paper; 箱- box
聚餐	jùcān	*n.* dinner party; *v.* have a dinner party 聚- to get together; 餐- meal
盘子	pánzi	*n.* plate
笨	bèn	*adj.* stupid
丢人	diūrén	*colloq.* embarrassing; *v.* lose face 丢- to lose, to throw
明明	míngmíng	*adv.* clearly, obviously

4 Everything is Fine 一切都很好

妻子	qīzi	*n.* wife (husband- 丈夫 zhàngfu)
玉红	Yùhóng	*n.* a woman's name 玉- jade; 红- red
帮忙	bāngmáng	*adj.* helpful; *v.* help 帮- to help, to assist; 忙- busy
捣蛋	dǎodàn	*v.* make trouble 捣- to smash; 蛋- egg
舒适	shūshì	*adj.* comfortable, cosy 舒- comfortable; 适- comfortable
热情	rèqíng	*adj.* warm, hospitable, enthusiastic 热- hot; 情- sentiment
相信	xiāngxìn	*v.* believe 相- [xiāng] each other, [xiàng] appearance; 信- to believe
一阵子	yízhènzi	*colloq.* a while, a short period of time
傍晚	bàngwǎn	*n.* dusk, early evening 傍- to be close to; 晚- evening
温水游泳池	wēnshuǐ yóuyǒngchí	*n.* heated pool 温- warm
太阳能	tàiyángnéng	*n.* solar energy 太阳- sun; 能- energy, to be able to
加温	jiāwēn	*v.* heat 加- to add; 温- warm

并(不)	bìng(bù)	*adv.* (not) at all [used before a negative word for emphasis] e.g. 汉语并不难学
耗电	hàodiàn	*v.* consume a lot of electricity 耗- to consume; 电- electricity
仍然	réngrán	*adv.* still
特有	tèyǒu	*adj.* peculiar 特- special
喂	wèi	*v.* feed; *int.* hello
袋鼠	dàishǔ	*n.* kangaroo 袋- bag; 鼠- mouse, rat
考拉	kǎolā	*n.* koala [transliteration] called 无尾熊 wúwěixióng in Taiwan 无- no, without; 尾- tail; 熊- bear
据说	jùshuō	it is said, allegedly 据- according to; 说- to speak
几乎	jīhū	*adv.* almost
一生	yìshēng	*adv.* throughout one's life
桉树	ānshù	*n.* eucalyptus tree
叶	yè	*n.* foliage, leaf
稀有	xīyǒu	*adj.* scarce, unusual 稀- scarce
国际	guójì	*adj.* international 国- nation, country; 际- inter-, between, among e.g. 校际- interschool
受	shòu	*v.* receive
保护	bǎohù	*v.* protect; *n.* protection 保- to keep, to protect; 护- to protect
各处	gèchù	*adv.* every place 各- every; 处- place
走走	zǒuzou	*v.* travel around, walk around
歌剧院	gējùyuàn	*n.* opera house 歌剧- opera; 院- a public place, yard
大堡礁	Dàbǎojiāo	*n.* Great Barrier Reef 堡- fort; 礁- reef
艾尔岩	Àiěryán	*n.* Ayers Rock (Uluru) 艾尔- Ayers [transliteration]; 岩- rock
照顾	zhàogù	*v.* look after, take care of
表现	biǎoxiàn	*v.* behave; *n.* behaviour
专心	zhuānxīn	*v.* concentrate; *adj.* attentive, absorbed 专- to engross
打瞌睡	dǎ kēshuì	*v.* doze off
用心	yòngxīn	*adj.* attentive, diligent 用- to use; 心- heart
环境	huánjìng	*n.* environment 环- to surround; 境- place, area
电	diàn	*n.* electricity
堪培拉	Kānpéilā	*n.* Canberra [transliteration]
珀斯	Pòsī	*n.* Perth [transliteration]
阿德莱德	Ādéláidé	*n.* Adelaide [transliteration]
苏东坡	Sū Dōngpō	*n.* a famous man of letters in Song dynasty
宋代	Sòngdài	*n.* Song dynasty (960 - 1279 AD)
文学家	wénxuéjiā	*n.* writer, person of letters 文学- literature; 家- [as a suffix] designating the specialty of a person, e.g. 科学家- scientist
回头	huítóu	*v.* turn one's head, turn around 回- to turn around; 头- head
有学问	yǒuxuéwèn	*adj.* knowledgeable 学问- knowledge
鼎鼎大名	dǐngdǐng dàmíng	*adj.* well-known, famous, celebrated
请上坐	qǐng shàngzuò	please have the best seat 上 - upper, better; 坐- to sit
副	fù	*m.w.* pair
对联	duìlián	*n.* a Chinese couplet written on scrolls etc. 对- pair, correct; 联- couplet
心情	xīnqíng	*n.* mood 心- heart; 情- sentiment
认识	rènshi	*v.* know, recognize 认- to recognize; 识- to know

2

学 写 字

换 huàn *to exchange*	决 jué *to decide*	定 dìng *to decide; certain*	方 fāng *method, place*	把 bǎ *[grammatical word]*
父 fù *father*	母 mǔ *mother*	亲 qīn *related by blood*	直 zhí *continuously; straight*	停 tíng *to stop*
聊 liáo *to chat*	简 jiǎn *simple*	单 dān *single; list*	希 xī *to hope*	望 wàng *to expect*
惯 guàn *to get used to*	餐 cān *meal*	肉 ròu *meat*	烤 kǎo *to toast, to grill, to bake*	牛 niú *ox, cow*
泡 pào *to brew(coffee/tea)*	知 zhī *to know*	道 dào *way, road; to say*	或 huò *or*	慢 màn *slow*
米 mǐ *rice*	准 zhǔn *standard, accurate*	备 bèi *to prepare*	收 shōu *to collect*	拾 shí *to pick up*
封 fēng *[m.w. for letter]*	信 xìn *letter (mail); to believe*	爱 ài *to love; love*	各 gè *every, each*	处 chù *place*

第三课 zhèng líng huā 挣零花钱

1 Feeling Great （感觉真好）

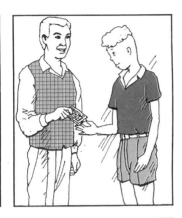

Listen and discuss -

1. What has become popular in the class lately and why?
2. What jobs are available?
3. What job does Xiaoming have? What are the working hours?
4. What transport does Xiaoming take to and from work?
5. How does Xiaoming feel about having a part-time job?

（一）感觉真好

最近，我们班上正在流行打工。大家都在工作，挣零花钱。

当然，有时候同学们难免要一起去看场电影，或打场保龄球什么的。每一次去玩儿都要花不少钱。不过，老是跟父母亲要钱，也是挺过意不去的。如果自己能挣点零花钱，就方便多了。

打工的方式很多，快餐店和咖啡馆常招服务员，地方报纸也常招送报员。只要肯做，是不难找到工作的。

我上个月在一家快餐店找到一份工作，每个星期做十二个小时，工作时间是星期一、三、五，下午三点半到七点半。时间安排得还不错，我三点下了课，走路到那里，把制服换下来，刚好开始工作。七点半下班以后，姐姐来接我回家。

有时候，我回到家里累得什么事都不想做。不过，工作虽然累，但是回报还不错。昨天妈妈临时需要用钱，我因为刚领了工资，就给了她五十块。妈妈很高兴，给了我一个拥吻。当时的感觉真好！

资 料 箱

● 他为什么打工？

他想挣零花钱。

想挣零花钱

想帮父母挣钱

想增加工作经验 (zēng)

在家无聊 (wú)

觉得好玩儿

● 他怎么打工？

他当送报员。

在快餐店当服务员 (wù yuán)

在咖啡馆当服务员 (kā fēi / wù yuán)

在餐馆当服务员

在服饰店当店员 (shì)

在书店当店员

在唱片行当店员 (háng)

在水果店当店员

当送报员 (bào)

当保姆 (bǎo mǔ)

● 这些是什么广告？ (guǎnggào)

招 店 员
服饰店招店员
外向，会说普通话
年龄： 十五岁～二十六岁
时间： 星期四下午五时～八时
星期六上午九时～下午三时
工资： 每小时十七元
电话： 9876 5432

保 姆
招保姆，照顾两岁小孩
喜欢小孩，有经验，大学或高中生。
时间： 每星期五下午六时～星期日上午十一时
工资： 每周一百五十元。
来信请寄： 打工路 1 2 3 号

读后讨论

1. 你打过工吗？为什么打工？做的是什么工作？

2. 你喜欢打什么工？为什么？

3. 你的朋友打工吗？在哪儿打工？为什么打工？

4. 你觉得工作好找吗？为什么？

5. 你觉得最好的打工时间是什么时候？为什么？

6. 你觉得打工的回报（bào）怎么样？

7. 在五十一页（yè）的两个广告（guǎnggào）中，哪个工作比较适合（shì hé）你？为什么？

挣来的

1

🕐 我们星期六去看电影，怎么样？

🕐 不行，我的零花钱用完（wán）了。

2

🕐 你打工的工资（zī）呢？

🕐 都给了我父母亲了。

3

🕐 你真是好孩子。你一个星期有多少零花钱？

🕐 我有五块钱。你呢？

4

🕐 我父母没给我零花钱，我的钱都是挣来的。

🕐 你没有打工，怎么挣钱？

5

🕐 我妈妈说，我如果吃了早饭再上学，她那天就付（fù）我二十块。……

6

🕐 ……我这个星期有三天吃了早饭，一共挣了六十块。

2 **Really Unbearable**（真受不了）

Listen and discuss -

1. Who of Dawei's friends are working? And where do they work?
2. How does Lanlan like her job?
3. How are Li Qiu's working conditions?
4. What was Dawei's work experience?
5. Do you think Lanlan will quit her job? Justify your answer.

（二） 真受不了

大伟，最近很多人都在打工，你知道吗？

我知道。小明在一家快餐店工作，李秋在一家咖啡馆当服务员。听说你也在餐馆找到了一份工作。那儿的工作环境怎么样？

不太好。因为顾客多半吸烟，餐馆里到处都是烟味，我真受不了。

李秋呢？她的工作怎么样？

那家咖啡馆的工作环境还不错。那儿因为不让吸烟，所以他们不用吸二手烟。她说她的老板人很客气，很照顾员工，顾客的态度也很好。那份工作虽然工资不高，但是她挺喜欢的。

李秋的运气不错。我的运气就没那么好。去年暑假我曾经在一家杂货店工作，那儿不但工资低，而且工作环境也差。

是吗？

是啊！那家杂货店又脏又乱，店的旁边就是酒馆，常常有喝醉酒的客人进去闹事。那儿的顾客也常把东西藏起来不付钱，或是把东西用坏了再拿回去退钱。

我的天，那真让人受不了。

更受不了的是老板很凶，一天到晚发脾气，所以我只做了两个星期就把工作辞掉了。

那种工作辞掉也好。我也真想把我那份工作辞掉，不过因为工资不错，辞掉很可惜。

资 料 箱

这儿的工作环境怎么样？

这儿老板很照顾员工。

老板人挺好的
老板人很客气
老板很照顾员工 (yuán)
老板凶得不得了 (xiōng)
顾客态度很好
顾客态度很差
顾客常吸烟，空气不好
又脏又乱 (zāng luàn)
又热，空气又差

你为什么把工作辞掉？(cí diào)

因为我做得太累了。

老板很凶 (xiōng)
顾客的态度很差
工作环境很差
我做得太累了
我功课太忙了 (gōng)

什么事最让你受不了？

我最受不了的是老板发脾气。

老板发脾气 (pí)
顾客态度差
老师太凶 (xiōng)
考试太多
作业太多
空气太差
电脑死机 (sǐ)
二手烟

读后讨论

1. 你喜欢什么样的工作环境?

2. 你吸过二手烟吗? 感觉怎么样?

3. 如果有人在你面前吸烟，你怎么办?

4. 你常发脾气吗? 为什么?
   <small>pí</small>

5. 如果你的老板很凶? 你怎么办?
   <small>xiōng</small>

6. 你看到过态度差的顾客吗? 当时的感觉怎么样?

7. 你遇到过哪些让你受不了的事?
   <small>yù</small>

退钱

☺ 对不起，我有东西要退钱。
<small>tuì</small>

☹ 有收据吗?
<small>shōu jù</small>
☺ 有，都在这儿。

☹ 好吧!你要退什么东西?
<small>tuì</small>
☺ 我要退这些……
<small>tuì</small>

☺ 这件衬衫现在太小了。
<small>chèn shān</small>

☺ 这条裤子现在太短了。
<small>kù</small>

☺ 这顶帽子式样不好看。
<small>dǐng mào　shì</small>

☺ 这双鞋……太旧了。
<small>shuāng xié</small>

yóu yù

3 A Long Hesitation（犹豫了半天）

Listen and discuss -

1. How does Xiaoming manage his part-time work earnings?
2. What did Xiaoming decide to buy and why did he make such a choice?
3. When did he go shopping and who did he go with?
4. What shop attracted them and why?
5. What was the decision Xiaoming had to make that day?
6. Describe Xiaoming's decision-making process. What are the pros and cons?

（三）犹豫了半天

从我开始打工到现在已经一个多月了。挣来的钱，我除了零花以外，剩下的就存起来。现在我已经存了一百多块钱了。我打算用这些钱去买个随身听，因为妈妈常唠叨，说我摇滚乐的声音开得太大、太吵。如果有随身听，我就不用担心吵到别人了。

星期五下课后，我找了几个同学一起去逛街。我们经过一家流行服饰店，里面摇滚乐的声音很大，大家就走了进去。这家服饰店卖的都是名牌衣服，价钱都很贵。我们各自拿了几件衣服试穿。我试穿了一件上衣和一条裤子，觉得还挺不错的。同学们也都说我看起来很酷。我很动心，可是又有点儿犹豫。买这么贵的衣服，妈妈一定会唠叨半天；而且，买了衣服，就没钱买随身听了。不过，这衣服料子好，颜色和式样又都是最流行的，我实在很喜欢，同学们也一直怂恿我买。犹豫了半天，最后我选择了买衣服。随身听只好等以后再买了，妈妈唠叨也就让她唠叨了。

资料箱

如果你存了钱，你最想做什么？

我想买一个随身听。

买一个随身听

买一部电脑

买名牌衣服

买游戏光盘

去中国旅行

存更多钱

你买衣服都怎么选择？

我选名牌的。

名牌的

式样流行的

颜色好看的

料子好的

看起来很酷的

穿起来舒服的

便宜的

他的父母常唠叨些什么？

他们最常唠叨的是他音乐声音开得太大。

音乐声音开得太大

房间太乱

花太多钱

整天玩电脑，看电视

学习不认真

考试前开夜车

睡觉太晚

早上起不来

一天到晚往外跑

车开得太快

读后讨论

1. 如果你存了钱，你最想做什么？
2. 你听音乐的时候喜欢把声音(shēng)开得很大吗？为什么？
3. 你喜欢随身(suí shēn)听吗？为什么？
4. 你逛街(guàng)时，什么东西最容易让你动心？
5. 你喜欢名牌衣服吗？为什么？
6. 你买衣服可以有自己的选择(zé)吗？你选些什么？
7. 你父母常唠叨吗？都唠叨些什么？

4 Not surprised at all （一点都不惊讶）
jīng yà

Listen and discuss –

1. What was the reason for the dinner party? And who attended?
2. Why weren't people surprised that Dawei received the scholarship?
3. Where is Dawei going and for how long? What change does Lanlan expect to see when he comes back?
4. What did they have for dinner and how did they enjoy it?

（四）一点都不惊讶（jīng yà）

二〇〇一年八月二十五日　星期六　天气阴转晴（yīn zhuǎn qíng）

　　再过两个星期大伟就要去中国了。今天晚上大家聚（jù）餐，给他饯（jiàn）行。参加聚（jù）餐的有十几个人，都是我们班上要好的同学，只可惜（xī）李秋刚（gāng）好要上班，没能参加。李秋说，这就是打工的坏处。

　　这一次大伟拿到奖（jiǎng）学金，我们一点都不惊讶（jīng yà）。他暑假去中国旅行，在北京交了一个朋友，回来后还常和他通（tōng）信。今年大伟一直想找个机会再去中国，刚好学校有一份去北京当交换学生的奖（jiǎng）学金，他就马上申（shēn）请了。大伟的学习成绩（jī）好，那份奖（jiǎng）学金就被（bèi）他拿到了。他这次要去一年。我相信一年以后回来，他的普通（pǔ tōng）话会说得非常流利。

　　今天的聚（jù）餐，大家都点了"任（rèn）你吃到饱（bǎo）"。这对男生来说很划（huá）算，因为他们胃（wèi）口大，吃得多。吃饭时，同学们一直用果汁敬（zhī jìng）大伟，祝他一切顺（shùn）利，还有人开玩笑地要他"干杯（gān bēi）"。这一餐，大家都吃得很开心。

资 料 箱

他们怎么给朋友饯(jiàn)行？

他们去饮茶楼饮茶。

去餐馆聚(jù)餐

去公园烤肉

去咖啡(kā fēi)馆聊天儿

去饮茶楼饮茶

去同学家开舞(wǔ)会

打工的坏处有哪些？

玩的时间少了。

学习的时间少了

玩的时间少了

很多活动都不能参加

很累

我们怎么祝福(fú)他人？

祝你一路顺风。

一路顺(shùn)风

旅途(tú yú)愉快

圣诞(shèng dàn)快乐

新年快乐

生日快乐

读后讨论

1. 你常和朋友聚餐吗？为什么聚餐？都在哪儿聚餐？

2. 你在班上有几个要好的朋友？你们在一起做什么？

3. 你认为打工有坏处吗？为什么？

4. 你在中国有朋友吗？有机会的话想不想交一个？

5. 你普通话说得流利吗？

6. 你打算去中国学习吗？有什么计划？

7. 你喜欢"任你吃到饱"吗？为什么？

例 句

1 **Feeling Great　感觉真好**

流行　**popular, in fashion**
这首歌最近非常流行。^{shǒu}
今年很流行红色的衣服。^{sè}
现在男生流行戴耳环。^{dài}
这种鞋现在很流行。^{xié}

难免　**[nánmiǎn] unavoidable, inevitable**
同学们在一起，难免要互相请客。^{hù}
出去逛街，难免要花钱。^{guàng}
交女朋友，难免要请她看电影。
一个人难免会做错事情。^{qíng}

老是　**always** It is usually used when things are unwelcomed.
他老是跟父母要钱。
他怎么老是忘了带作业？
你为什么上课老是迟到？^{chí}

跟　　(1) **towards, with (someone/something)** It introduces the relevant target of an action.
他又跟父母吵架了。^{chǎo jià}
他又跟姐姐借钱了。^{jiè}
这件事你最好不要跟老师说。

　　　(2) **and, with**
我弟弟跟我都喜欢打网球。
明天你跟我一块儿去吧。

如果　**if, in case, in the event of** "如果" is often followed by "就".
如果我们没赶上公共汽车，就得走路去。^{gǎn}
如果下午不下雨，我们就去游泳。
如果你晚上早点儿睡觉，早上就不会起不来。^{shuì}
如果你不喜欢的话，就不要买。

只要　**as long as, provided**
只要你肯做，是不难找到工作的。^{kěn} ^{nán}
只要你肯用功，考试一定考得好。^{kěn} ^{gōng}
只要不下雨，我们就可以走路去。

2　Really Unbearable　真受不了

受不了　**cannot endure/stand, unbearable**

我的老板很凶，真让人受不了。

这儿都是烟味，我受不了。

他老是迟到，真让人受不了。

爸爸的书房又脏又乱，妈妈很受不了。

曾经　**once, ever, formerly**　It is used to indicate a past experience.

去年我曾经在一家杂货店打工。

我曾经见过她两次。

我曾经在上海住了两年。

不但……而且……　**not only... but also**

这儿不但老板人好，而且顾客的态度也好。

她不但长得漂亮，而且家里也很有钱。

这件衣服不但好看，而且也很便宜。

他不但教学认真，而且也很关心学生。

她不但人缘儿好，而且学习也好。

v + 起来　(1) **indicate an upward action**

请大家站起来。

(2) **indicate a put-away, put-aside action**

他把好吃的东西藏起来。

把那本书藏起来，别让老师看到。

天气热了，妈妈把冬天的衣服收起来了。

(3) **express an impression or opinion**

那件旗袍她穿起来很好看。

他今天看起来不太高兴。

也好　**may as well, may not be a bad idea**

他要试，让他试试也好。

反正有空，去逛逛街也好。

那份工作的工资太差了，不做也好。

雨下得这么大，我看你不去也好。

可惜　**it's a pity**

这些衣服还挺好的，丢掉很可惜。

大家都要去看电影，只可惜我不能去。

星期六有一场音乐会，可惜我没空参加。

我觉得你把那份工作辞掉很可惜。

3　A Long Hesitation　犹 豫 了 半 天

唠叨　[láodāo] **to nag**

我妈妈常唠叨，说我的房间太乱^{luàn}了。

姐姐一天到晚唠叨，我真受不了。

如果我太晚回家，我妈妈就唠叨半天。

好了，我知道了，别^{bié}再唠叨了。

各自　**respectively**

今天逛街时，我们各自买了一件名牌衣服。

老师在上课，同学们却各自做自己的事。

下课后同学们都各自忙着自己的活动。

动心　**heart set on (something or someone)**

店里那件黄色^{sè}的连^{lián}衣裙^{qún}很好看，我实^{shí}在很动心。

我看，他对我姐姐很动心。

店员一直怂恿^{sǒng yǒng}他买，但他就是不动心。

犹豫　[yóuyù] **hesitate, be undecided**

他在犹豫，是不是要去打工。

他想请她看电影，可是又有点儿犹豫。

赶^{gǎn}快决定吧！不要再犹豫了。

她犹豫了半天才加入我们的足球队。

怂恿　[sǒngyǒng] **urge, push or tempt**　It is used when urging someone to do what he is not supposed to do.

我还不到十五岁，可是他一直怂恿我去看成人电影。

他最近一直怂恿我弟弟吸烟。

他老是怂恿别人做不该做的事。

而且　**also**　而且 is often used following 不但, but can also be used on its own.

这些苹^{píng}果很好吃，而且也不贵。

那家杂^{zá}货^{huò}店的老板很凶^{xiōng}，而且顾客的态度也很差。

他不但人很好，而且做事也很认真。

黄老师不但教学认真，而且也很关心学生。

只好　**have no choice but to, have to**

好吃的东西都吃完了，我只好吃面包。

我的零花钱用完^{wán}了，只好向姐姐借^{jiè}。

我今天没赶^{gǎn}上车，只好走路回家。

3

4　Not surprised at all　一点都不惊讶

再过　**another**　This is usually followed by a length of time or distance.

再过两天就是我的生日了。

再过一个星期就是圣诞节了。
（shèng dàn）

再过两站就到动物园了。

再过半年我就二十岁了。

给……饯行　**to give somebody a farewell party**

章老师要回中国了，我们给他饯行吧！
（Zhāng）　　　　　　　　　　（jiàn）

昨天晚上同学们在饮茶楼聚餐，给汉语老师饯行。
（jù）　　　　　　　　　　　　　（jiàn）

我们晚上给小张的饯行，你去不去？

要好　**good (friendship), close (friendship)**

他在班上有很多要好的朋友。

他是我最要好的朋友。

小高和他很要好。

被　[bèi]　(passive signifier) It is placed before the verb to indicate how the subject is conducted.

他拿到了那份奖学金。　　那份奖学金被他拿到了。
（jiǎng）　　　　　　　　　　（jiǎng）

姐姐吃了我的巧克力。　　我的巧克力被姐姐吃了。
（qiǎo kè）　　　　　　　　（qiǎo kè）

哥哥开走了爸爸的车。　　爸爸的车被哥哥开走了。

昨天老师骂他了。　　　　昨天他被老师骂了。
（mà）　　　　　　　　　　（mà）

对……来说　**as for ...**

去餐厅点"任你吃到饱"，对男生来说很划算。
（tīng）　　　　　　　　　　　　　　（huá）

这个问题，对他来说真是太容易了。
（róng yì）

考试对学生来说是一件大事。

划算　[huásuàn]　**worth the cost, worth it**

今天我买了两件衣服，是买一送一，真划算。

这一餐大家都吃得很过瘾，一共才花二十块，真划算。
（yǐn）

这件衣服料子不好，花那么多钱不划算。
（liào）

你胃口小，吃"任你吃到饱"不划算。
（wèi）

胃口　[wèikǒu]　**appetite**

今天妈妈很高兴，胃口很好。

我今天不舒服，没什么胃口。

他今天胃口不好，吃得很少。

生 词

---

1 Feeling Great 感 觉 真 好

挣	zhèng	*v.* earn, make (money)
零花钱	línghuāqián	*n.* pocket money 零- small amount, zero; 花- to spend, flower
感觉	gǎnjué	*n.* feeling; *v.* feel 感- to feel, feeling; 觉- to feel
流行	liúxíng	*adj.* popular, in fashion 流- to flow; 行- to walk, to travel
打工	dǎgōng	*v.* have a part-time job 打- to hit; 工- work, job
难免	nánmiǎn	*adj.* inevitable, unavoidable 难- difficult; 免- to avoid
保龄球	bǎolíngqiú	*n.* bowling [transliteration] 保- to keep, to protect; 龄- age
什么的	shénmede	*colloq.* and so on, and so forth
花	huā	*v.* spend, e.g. 花钱- to spend money; *n.* flower
老是	lǎoshì	*adv.* always, all the time
跟	gēn	*prep.* towards or with, e.g. 跟父母要钱; *conj.* and, e.g. 他跟我是好朋友。
要	yào	*v.* ask for, want
过意不去	guòyì búqù	*v.* feel guilty about
方式	fāngshì	*n.* way 方- method, place; 式- style
快餐店	kuàicāndiàn	*n.* fast-food restaurant 快- fast; 餐- meal; 店- shop, store
咖啡馆	kāfēiguǎn	*n.* coffee shop 咖啡- coffee; 馆- building, shop
招	zhāo	*v.* recruit
服务员	fúwùyuán	*n.* waiter, waitress 服- to serve; 务- affair, business; 员- personnel
地方	dìfāng	*adj.* local; *n.* place, location
送报员	sòngbàoyuán	*n.* newsboy 送- to deliver; 报- newspaper; 员- personnel
肯	kěn	*v.* be willing to
安排	ānpái	*v.* arrange 安- to find a suitable place for; 排- to line up
制服	zhìfú	*n.* uniform 制- to restrict, system; 服- clothes
换	huàn	*v.* change, exchange
回报	huíbào	*n.* return, reward
临时	línshí	*adv.* at the time (when something happens)
领	lǐng	*v.* get, receive (money or prize)
工资	gōngzī	*n.* salary, wage 工- work, job; 资- money
拥吻	yōngwěn	*n.* hug and kiss 拥- hug, to hug; 吻- kiss, to kiss
当时	dāngshí	*adv.* at that time, then 当- at the time; to serve, to be
经验	jīngyàn	*n.* experience 经- to go through; 验- to check
服饰店	fúshìdiàn	*n.* fashion shop 服- clothes; 饰- ornament
店员	diànyuán	*n.* clerk, salesperson 店- shop, store; 员- personnel
唱片行	chàngpiànháng	*n.* music store 唱片- disk; 行- business firm
保姆	bǎomǔ	*n.* baby-sitter, nanny
广告	guǎnggào	*n.* advertisement
适合	shìhé	*v.* suit; *adj.* suitable
付	fù	*v.* pay

2 Really Unbearable　真受不了

受不了	shòu bu liǎo	*colloq.* cannot endure or stand; unbearable
餐馆	cānguǎn	*n.* restaurant 餐- meal; 馆- building, shop
环境	huánjìng	*n.* environment 环- to surround, ring, hoop; 境- place, area
顾客	gùkè	*n.* customer, client 顾- to attend to; 客- guest
吸烟	xīyān	*v.* smoke 吸- to inhale; 烟- cigarette, smoke
到处	dàochù	*adv.* everywhere 到- to reach, to go to; 处- place
烟味	yānwèi	*n.* cigarette smell 烟- cigarette, smoke; 味- smell
二手烟	èrshǒuyān	*n.* passive smoking 二手- second-hand
老板	lǎobǎn	*n.* boss 老- old; 板- board
人	rén	*n.* personality, personal features, usually followed by a description, e.g. 人很好- of a good personality; 人很客气- be a polite person; 人很高- be a tall person
员工	yuángōng	*n.* employee
态度	tàidù	*n.* attitude 态- attitude; 度- degree
运气	yùnqì	*n.* luck 运- luck, to transport; 气- air
曾经	céngjīng	*adv.* once, formerly, ever
杂货店	záhuòdiàn	*n.* grocery store 杂- sundry, miscellaneous; 货- goods, merchandise
不但	búdàn	*conj.* not only
而且	érqiě	*conj.* also, moreover, in addition 而- yet; 且- also, moreover
差	chà	*adj.* not up to standard, poor; *v.* differ (by), be short
脏	zāng	*adj.* dirty
乱	luàn	*adj.* messy
酒馆	jiǔguǎn	*n.* bar, pub 酒- alchoholic drink; 馆- building, shop
喝酒	hējiǔ	*v.* drink wine/liquor 喝醉酒- get drunk; 醉- *adj.* drunk
闹事	nàoshì	*v.* make trouble, create a disturbance 闹- to create disturbances; 事- matter, affairs
藏	cáng	*v.* hide
起来	qǐlai	*suffix,* see p. 66
付	fù	*v.* pay
退	tuì	*v.* return (things) 退钱- to get/give a refund; 退东西- to return things
脾气	píqi	*n.* temper 发脾气- to lose temper
辞掉	cídiào	*v.* quit, resign, sack 辞- to resign; 掉- [a particle] away, out
也好	yěhǎo	*phr.* may as well, may not be a bad idea
可惜	kěxī	it's a pity, too bad 可- to approve, can, may; 惜- to have pity on
死机	sǐjī	*v.* break down (computer) 死- to die, dead; 机- machine
收据	shōujù	*n.* receipt 收- to collect; 据- proof
式样	shìyàng	*n.* style 式- style; 样- pattern
试	shì	*v.* try
丢掉	diūdiào	*v.* throw away 丢- to throw, to lose; 掉- [a particle] away, out

3 A Long Hesitation　犹豫了半天

犹豫	yóuyù	*v.* hesitate, be undecided
从	cóng	*adv.* since, from
零花	línghuā	*v.* spend pocket money

剩下	shèngxià	v. remain, be left 剩- remain, be left
存	cún	v. save, deposit
随身听	suíshēntīng	n. walkman 随- to follow; 身- body; 听- to listen
唠叨	láodāo	v. nag 唠- talkative; 叨- talkative
声音	shēngyīn	n. sound, voice
吵	chǎo	adj. noisy; v. disturb, quarrel
别人	biérén	n. other people
服饰店	fúshìdiàn	n. fashion shop 服- clothes; 饰- ornament
各自	gèzì	adv. respectively
试穿	shìchuān	v. try on (clothes/shoes) 试- to try; 穿- to wear, to put on
名牌	míngpái	n. famous brand 名- famous, name; 牌- brand, plate, sign
价钱	jiàqián	n. price
上衣	shàngyī	n. upper garment 上- upper, on, to go to; 衣- clothes
酷	kù	slang cool [transliteration]; cruel, extreme
动心	dòngxīn	adj. heart set on (something or someone)
料子	liàozi	n. material (fabric)
颜色	yánsè	n. colour 颜- colour; 色- colour
式样	shìyàng	n. style 式- style; 样- pattern
实在	shízài	adv. really 实- real, true, actual; 在- at, in, on, exist
怂恿	sǒngyǒng	v. urge, push, tempt
小卖部	xiǎomàibù	n. tuck-shop, canteen 小- little; 卖- sale, to sell; 部- section, unit

4 Not surprised at all 一 点 都 不 惊 讶

饯行	jiànxíng	v. give a farewell party 饯- to give a farewell party; 行- to travel
聚餐	jùcān	v. have a dinner party 聚- to get together; 餐- meal
要好	yàohǎo	adj. good (friendship), close (friendship)
坏处	huàichù	n. disadvantage, drawback 坏- bad; 处- point, part, place
奖学金	jiǎngxuéjīn	n. scholarship 奖- to reward, an award; 学- study; 金- money, gold
惊讶	jīngyà	adj. surprised 惊- to surprise, shock; 讶- to be surprised
通信	tōngxìn	v. correspond 通- through, to get through; 信- letter
申请	shēnqǐng	v. apply for
成绩	chéngjī	n. achievement, result 成- to become, to succeed; 绩- achievement
被	bèi	passive signifier, see p. 68
流利	liúlì	adj. fluent 流- to flow; 利- smoothly
任你吃到饱	rèn nǐ chī dào bǎo	all you can eat 任- to let, to allow; 饱- full
对……来说	duì...lái shuō	as for...
划算	huásuàn	adj. worth the cost, worth it
胃口	wèikǒu	n. appetite 胃- stomach; 口- mouth
敬	jìng	v. propose a toast, offer politely
顺利	shùnlì	adv. smoothly, successfully 顺- smooth; 利- smoothly
干杯	gānbēi	colloq. bottoms up 干- to dry; 杯- glass, cup
餐	cān	n. meal
祝福	zhùfú	v. offer good wishes 祝- to wish; 福- luck, happiness

3

学写字

流 liú *to flow*	工 gōng *work, job*	挣 zhèng *to earn, to make (money)*	零 líng *small amount; zero*	花 huā *to spend; flower*
跟 gēn *towards, with, and*	挺 tǐng *quite*	如 rú *if*	果 guǒ *result, fruit*	店 diàn *shop*
馆 guǎn *shop, building*	份 fèn *[m.w. for job, report]*	累 lèi *tired*	受 shòu *to bear; to receive*	环 huán *to surround; ring, hoop*
境 jìng *area, place*	顾 gù *to attend to*	吸 xī *to inhale*	烟 yān *cigarette, smoke*	板 bǎn *board*
态 tài *attitude*	运 yùn *luck; to transport*	而 ér *yet*	且 qiě *also, moreover*	酒 jiǔ *wine, liquor*
唠 láo *talkative*	叨 dāo *talkative*	名 míng *famous; name*	牌 pái *brand; plate, sign*	惜 xī *to have pity on*
刚 gāng *just now, just*	普 pǔ *general, universal*	通 tōng *through, to get through*	任 rèn *let, allow; official post*	饱 bǎo *full*

第四课　年轻人的世界

1 **Not a big deal** （没什么大不^{liǎo}了）

Listen and discuss -

1. What did Li Qiu do to Lanlan and why did she do that ?
2. What happened to Lanlan? Why did it happen?
3. What was Li Qiu's remark upon Lanlan's decision?
4. How did Lanlan justify her decision?
5. What was Li Qiu's opinion of Lanlan's mother? How did Lanlan respond to this comment?

（一）没什么大不了

嗨！！！

吓了我一跳！李秋。

对不起！你在想什么？发呆啊？

唉！本来是想看书的，可是才看了几页就看不下去了。

我看啊，你一定又在想你的那位英俊小生了。

别提他了，我们已经吹了。

你们吹了？是他交了新女朋友，还是你交了新男朋友？

都不是。因为我们俩个性差得太远，所以就决定分手了。

你不是在开玩笑吧？他个子高，人也帅，在球场上又最出风头，是每个女孩子心目中的白马王子呢！

我本来也是很崇拜他的，不过后来发现他非常骄傲，把别人都不放在眼里。前几天我们吵了一架，就决定分手了。

就这么分手，你不难过吗？

我是有点儿难过，不过分手就分手了，也没什么大不了的。哈！我妈妈可高兴了，因为她本来就不赞成我现在交男朋友。她认为交男朋友应该是上了大学以后的事。

我看你妈妈真不开通，交男朋友又不是什么大不了的事！

其实我想想，她说的也有道理。再过一年就要中学毕业了，现在得好好儿学习，将来才能进入好的大学。

资料箱

● 你看她在想什么？

^{kě shuì}
打瞌睡

^{dāi}
发呆

^{mèng}
做白日梦

^{wáng}
想她的白马王子

^{jùn}
想她的英俊小生

● 你希望你的男／女朋友是怎么样的人？

^{qīng xiù}
长得很清秀

长得很迷人

^{piào liàng}
又聪明又漂亮

^{pí}
脾气很好

^{yuán}
人缘儿很好

^{shuài}
长得很帅

^{zhuàng}
长得很 壮

个子很高

^{cháng}
在球场上很出风头

学习很好

● 他父母亲为什么不高兴？

回家太晚

吸烟

^{zuì}
喝醉酒

^{xì}
天天玩电子游戏

天天上网聊天

常常打电话聊天

花太多钱

学习不认真

读后讨论

1. 你常发呆吗？为什么？

2. 你认为个性差得远的人可以成为好朋友吗？为什么？

3. 你希望你的男／女朋友是怎么样的人？

4. 你对中学生交男／女朋友有什么看法？

5. 你父母亲赞成你现在交男／女朋友吗？为什么？

6. 你觉得你父母亲开通吗？为什么？

7. 中学毕业以后，你想上大学吗？为什么？

男朋友

听说你有好几个男朋友？

谁说的？没有这回事。

1

昨天和你走在一起的那个人是谁？

他是英英的男朋友。

2

今天早上和你说话的那个人是谁？

他是我的老师。

3

你不会离开我吧？

不会，我永远爱你。

4

时间不早了。走吧！妈，我送你回养老院去。

5

2 Just for fun（好玩而已）

Listen and discuss -

1. What was Li Qiu accusing Xiaoming of? What was the clue?
2. What was Xiaoming's attitude towards his own conduct?
3. What was Li Qiu's reaction towards this conduct?
4. What advice did Li Qiu offer?
5. What did Li Qiu plead for and how did Xiaoming respond to it?

（二）好玩而已

嘿！小明，你身上有烟味，是不是抽烟了？

没有啊！

说谎！我明明闻到烟味。快老实说来！

才抽一根而已啦！

学校规定不准抽烟，你是知道的。你哪儿来的香烟？

是一个十二年级的同学给我的。放心，没人看到。

没人看到也不行。抽烟对身体有害，一上瘾就麻烦了。你没看到昨天报纸上的消息吗？有一个大学生吸毒过量，差点儿死掉。

我看到了，那是吸毒。抽烟和吸毒是两回事，你干吗把它们扯到一起？

对不起，我是不应该把这两件事扯到一起。不过，你得知道，"吸烟容易，戒烟难"。

我知道，我只是抽着好玩而已，不会上瘾的。

说是这么说，问题是，抽烟很容易上瘾，就跟吸毒很容易上瘾一样。很多人刚开始吸毒也只是好玩而已，可是一旦上了瘾，想戒都戒不掉。

你看，你又把抽烟和吸毒扯到一起了。

对不起，我毛病又犯了。反正，抽不抽烟是在于你自己，我只是关心你而已。

好啦！好啦！我以后不抽了。真是的，小题大做！

资 料 箱

他为什么抽烟？

因为他认为看起来
很有派头。

好玩儿
朋友的怂恿 ^{sǒng yǒng}
他的朋友都抽烟
他认为看起来很酷 ^{kù}
他认为看起来很有派头 ^{pài}
他想忘掉不愉快的事情 ^{diào　yú}

抽烟和吸毒 ^{dú} 有什么坏处？

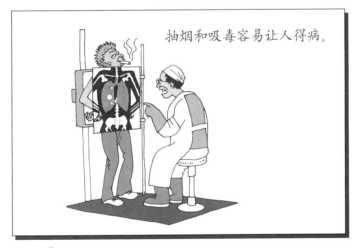

抽烟和吸毒容易让人得病。

对身体有害
会上瘾 ^{yǐn}
很浪费钱 ^{làng fèi}
容易让人犯罪 ^{fàn zuì}
容易让人得病

你常犯 ^{fàn} 什么毛病？

我常上课打瞌睡。

常惹父母生气 ^{rě}
常惹老师生气 ^{rě}
常上课打瞌睡 ^{kē shuì}
常花太多钱
老是忘了带作业
容易小题大做

读后讨论

1. 你对抽烟有什么看法？抽烟有什么坏处？
2. 你知道谁戒(jiè)过烟吗？经过怎么样？
3. 你对吸毒(dú)有什么看法？吸毒(dú)有什么坏处？
4. 如果有人怂恿(sǒng yǒng)你吸毒(dú)，你该怎么办？
5. 如果你知道你的朋友抽烟或吸毒(dú)，你怎么办？
6. 你常犯(fàn)什么毛病？

二手烟

两位先生，请进。

1

吸烟区(qū)还是非吸烟区(qū)？

非吸烟区　吸烟区

吸烟区。

2

这儿空气真差，到处都是烟味(wèi)。我们去非吸烟区(qū)吧。

不，我们还是坐这儿好。

3

为什么？你不是戒(jiè)烟了吗？

我是戒(jiè)了。

4

那你为什么选吸烟区(qū)呢？

5

因为医生只说不准(zhǔn)我吸烟，他没说不准我吸二手烟(yā)呀！

6

3 A little dilemma （有点儿矛盾）
máo dùn

Listen and discuss -

1. What did Li Qiu and her friends do this afternoon? How did she feel afterward?
2. What trouble did she have when she got home?
3. What happened later in the evening?
4. How did Li Qiu feel about her mother's reaction?
5. What did Li Qiu think of herself in terms of fashion?

（三）有点儿矛<ruby>盾<rt>máo dùn</rt></ruby>

　　今天下午我和班上的几个女孩子一起去<ruby>逛<rt>guàng</rt></ruby>街。<ruby>临<rt>lín</rt></ruby>时有人<ruby>提议<rt>tí yì</rt></ruby>去<ruby>染<rt>rǎn</rt></ruby>头发，大家都赞成，我们就进了美容院。我把前面两边的头发<ruby>染<rt>rǎn</rt></ruby>成了<ruby>紫<rt>zǐ</rt></ruby>色，我觉得看起来还不错。<ruby>染<rt>rǎn</rt></ruby>了头发后，大家走在路上，都觉得挺<ruby>特<rt>tè</rt></ruby>别，挺好玩儿的。这时，又有人<ruby>提议<rt>tí yì</rt></ruby>，要去穿肚<ruby>脐<rt>qí</rt></ruby>洞。我本来是不想去的，后来<ruby>禁<rt>jīn</rt></ruby>不起同学的<ruby>怂恿<rt>sǒng yǒng</rt></ruby>，也跟着去了。在肚<ruby>脐<rt>qí</rt></ruby>上<ruby>戴<rt>dài</rt></ruby>了个环以后，我心里觉得<ruby>怪<rt>guài</rt></ruby>怪的，不知道自己<ruby>究竟<rt>jiū jìng</rt></ruby>是喜欢还是不喜欢。

　　最大的问题是，回到家里，妈妈一看到我的头发就开始唠叨，说年<ruby>轻<rt>qīng</rt></ruby>人不好好儿学习，就会作怪。到了晚上，妹妹<ruby>偷<rt>tōu</rt></ruby>偷地把我<ruby>戴<rt>dài</rt></ruby>肚<ruby>脐<rt>qí</rt></ruby>环的事<ruby>告诉<rt>gào sù</rt></ruby>了妈妈。妈妈一听，<ruby>更<rt>gèng</rt></ruby>是大发<ruby>脾<rt>pí</rt></ruby>气。

　　我觉得妈妈实在太小题大做了。<ruby>染<rt>rǎn</rt></ruby>头发，<ruby>戴<rt>dài</rt></ruby>肚<ruby>脐<rt>qí</rt></ruby>环，只是<ruby>赶<rt>gǎn</rt></ruby>新<ruby>潮<rt>cháo</rt></ruby>，又不是<ruby>干<rt>gàn</rt></ruby>坏事。现在街上到处是新<ruby>潮<rt>cháo</rt></ruby>的年轻人，做各种奇怪的打<ruby>扮<rt>bàn</rt></ruby>，跟他们比起来，我是很<ruby>保守<rt>bǎo shǒu</rt></ruby>的了。妈妈是个挺开明的人，不知道为什么今天这么不开通。

　　老实说，<ruby>戴<rt>dài</rt></ruby>不<ruby>戴<rt>dài</rt></ruby>肚<ruby>脐<rt>qí</rt></ruby>环，我心里也有点儿矛<ruby>盾<rt>máo dùn</rt></ruby>。现在想想，<ruby>戴<rt>dài</rt></ruby>肚<ruby>脐<rt>qí</rt></ruby>环也挺不方便的，说不定过几天我就把它拿下来。

资料箱

你的朋友会怂恿(sǒng yǒng)你做什么？

他们会怂恿我染头发。

买流行的服饰(shì)

染(rǎn)头发

戴(dài)肚脐(qí)环

文身

抽烟

做奇怪的打扮(bàn)

年轻人常抱怨(bào yuàn)父母什么？

我爸爸是老古板。

Try this, Dad!

很不开通

是老古(gǔ)板

太保守(bǎo shǒu)

爱唠叨

常发脾(pí)气

不关心我

爱小题大做

不了(jiě)解年轻人的想法(fǎ)

他 / 她为什么心里觉得矛盾？

因为她要减肥，又想吃巧克力。

要减肥(jiǎn féi)，又想吃巧克力(qiǎo kè lì)

想存(cún)钱，又喜欢买名牌衣服

想染(rǎn)头发，又怕(pà)妈妈唠叨

想去旅行，又怕花钱

想打工，又怕(pà)忙不过来

读后讨论

1. 你对染(rǎn)头发有什么看法？你染(rǎn)不染头发？

2. 你曾(céng)经禁(jīn)不起同学的怂恿(sǒng yǒng)而做了你不该做的事吗？是什么事？

3. 你常临(lín)时决定做一件事吗？是什么事？

4. 你妈妈常跟你唠叨什么？

5. 你父母曾(céng)经跟你发脾(pí)气吗？为了什么？当时你的感觉怎么样？

6. 你觉得现在的年轻人很会作怪吗？为什么？。

7. 你觉得自己是新潮(cháo)的还是保守(bǎo shǒu)的？为什么？

8. 什么事曾(céng)经让你心里觉得矛盾(máo dùn)？

自相矛盾

1. 快来买矛(máo)，我的矛(máo)是世界(shì jiè)上最好的矛(máo)。

2. 你的矛(máo)有多好呢？

3. 可好呢！它可以刺(cì)穿任何(hé)东西。
真好！真好！

4. 快来买盾(dùn)，我的盾(dùn)是世界上最好的盾(dùn)！

5. 你的盾有多好呢？

6. 可好呢！没有任何(hé)东西可以刺(cì)穿它。
真好！真好！

7. 那么，如果拿你的矛来刺你的盾呢？
这，这…

4 **Unpleasant happenings** （不愉快的事）

Listen and discuss -

1. What's the source of the message, and where is it displayed?
2. What are the two unpleasant events encountered by Dawei? Give details.
3. What are Dawei's comments on students in China?
4. What often happens to Dawei on his way home from school, and why?
5. What does Dawei like to know about Xiaoming?

（四）不愉快的事

　　自从大伟去北京以后，小明常和他互相发电子邮件。昨天小明又接到一份大伟发来的邮件，就把它贴在他们班的网页上，让大家看。

小明：

　　我今天碰到两件不愉快的事：一件是买不到电影票，另一件是差点儿被车撞上。上午，我请班上的一个女同学陈英去看电影。我们很早就去排队买票，本来应该是可以买到票的，没想到前面一直有人插队，结果还没轮到我们，票就卖完了。你说气不气人？后来我们决定过马路去逛书店。就在我们过马路时，有一辆车开得非常快，差点儿撞上我，真把我吓坏了。在这儿，我最讨厌过马路了。十字路口虽然有红绿灯和人行横道，但车还是不让人。

　　好了，不谈不愉快的事了。今天陈英在书店买了数学和英语参考书。她说是买了回去自己在家里做练习。陈英非常用功，学习成绩很好。我发现这儿的学生都很用功。他们上课专心，不捣蛋。大家都认为把英语学好是很重要的。在我从学校回家的路上，就常常有年轻人跟我聊天，找机会练习英语。

　　你现在忙吗？还在打工吗？请代我向大家问好。

大伟

资料箱

你当时的感觉怎么样？

我当时很紧张。

有点儿犹豫 yóu yù
有点儿担心 dān
很紧张 jǐn
很生气
很放心
非常开心
非常高兴
非常难过
被吓坏了 xià

你最讨厌什么样的人或事？ tǎo yàn

我最讨厌的是有人插队。

有人插队 chā
坐不上公共汽车
车不让人
过马路
爱发脾气的人 pí
上课爱捣蛋的学生 dǎo dàn
骄傲的人 jiāo ào
爱出风头的人
不开通的父母

你怎么练习汉语？

我常和中国人聊天。

和中国人聊天
听汉语录音带 lù
听汉语CD
在电脑上学习
念课文
背生词 bèi cí

 读后讨论

1. 你最常看什么网页？为什么？

2. 你看电影曾经买不到票吗？当时的感觉怎么样？
^{céng}

3. 你曾经看到过有人插队吗？当时的感觉怎么样？

4. 你常逛书店吗？都买什么书？

5. 你平常怎么过马路？

6. 你最讨厌什么样的人或事？

7. 你怎么练习汉语？

【谜语】
^{mí}

1. 个子是又高又瘦，
   头发长在脚底下；
   年轻时是白头发，
   年老时是黑头发。

   － 打一物 －
^{wù}

2. 出去时常用它，
   在家时不用它；
   用它时不见它，
   见它时不用它。

   － 打一物 －
^{wù}

3. 我不是很有钱，
   也不是很漂亮；
   但只要我说了，
   你就一直想我。

   － 打一事 －

4. 虽然是你的，
   常给别人用；
   别人用它时，
   不用你同意。

   － 打一词 －
^{cí}

例句

1 Not a Big Deal 没什么大不了

大不了 **serious, big deal** It is often used in a negative form, e.g. 没什么大不了 - no big
deal; 不是什么大不了的事 - not serious business.

男朋友吹就吹了，没什么大不了的。

我只是得了小感冒，没什么大不了的。

吸烟又不是什么大不了的事，你别紧张。

下去 v + 得下去 When 下去 is used following a verb, it indicates an action being continued.

To indicate an action which is able to be carried on, v + 得下去 is used.

To indicate an action which is unable to be carried on, v + 不下去 is used.

这本书很没意思，你看得下去吗？

我看不下去，这本书太没意思了。

她难过得说不下去。

他太累了，功课做不下去了。

出风头 **be in the spotlight; show off**

他球打得好，在球场上很出风头。

他人缘儿好，学习又好，在学校很出风头。

她在班上很爱出风头。

心目中 **in one's eyes**

我弟弟是学校老师心目中的好学生。

他长得帅，是女孩子心目中的白马王子。

在大家的心目中，他是一个好爸爸。

把……都不放在眼里 **paying no respect to ...**

她很骄傲，把别人都不放在眼里。

他上课一直讲话，把老师都不放在眼里。

他们认为自己球打得很好，把我们都不放在眼里。

就 **(emphasizing word)** When "就" is used between two repeated verbs, it indicates
a suggestion of tolerating what has happened/will happen, or taking it with ease.

女朋友吹就吹了，不要难过了。

公共汽车没坐上就没坐上了，再等下一班吧！

工作辞掉就辞掉了，没什么可惜的。

4

Use of 才

    (1) **just; only**

        他才看了几页书就看不下去了。

        学校才开学，大家就忙得不得了。

        你今年才十四岁，还不可以开车。

    (2) **(only...) then**　It indicates something which depends upon a certain condition.

        你得好好儿念书，将来才能进入好的大学。

        你要早点儿回家，你妈妈才不会担心。

        多吃些，肚子才不会饿。

    (3) **as late as**　It indicates something has happened later than expected.

        大家都早就来了，你怎么现在才来？

        昨天的聚餐一点钟开始，可是他两点才到。

2　Just for Fun 好玩而已

明明　**clearly, obviously**　It is used to emphasize the authenticity of a fact. It is ofen

    followed by a outcome which is opposite to that fact.

    我明明闻到烟味，你却说你没有抽烟。

    我明明听到有人说话，怎么没看到人？

    天气预报明明说今天会是晴天，谁知道却下了大雨。

    他明明说今天要来的，不知道为什么没来。

到　**v + 到**　When used after a verb, 到 indicates the achievement of an action.

    你说你没抽烟，可是我明明闻到烟味。

    我在跟你说话，你听到了吗？

    他在球场旁边找到了他的书包。

    他拿到了那份奖学金。

老实说来　**to speak out honestly**

    你是不是抽烟了？老实说来！

    你到底有没有女朋友？老实说来！

    那件事你做了没？老实说来！

而已　**that's all**　It is often used together with "才", "只是" or words of similar meaning.

    我才抽了一根烟而已，别小题大做了。

    我只是开玩笑而已，你不要生气。

    我只是上网聊天而已，我妈妈就唠叨了半天。

    放心，我抽烟只是好玩而已，不会上瘾的。

规定　[guīdìng] **to stipulate**

学校规定学生不准抽烟。

学校规定学生上学要穿制服。 <small>zhì</small>

爸爸规定我今天十点钟以前回家。 <small>zhōng</small>

干吗　[gànmá]　**why on earth, whatever for**

想吃就说，干吗不好意思？

这些事情你自己都知道，干吗还问我？ <small>qíng</small>

想请我哥哥看电影就请他去，干吗找我一块儿去？

小题大做　**make a mountain out of a molehill**

那个人的毛病是喜欢小题大做。

我只迟到五分钟他就大发脾气，真是小题大做。 <small>chí　zhōng　pí</small>

戴五个耳环又不是什么大不了的事，别小题大做了。 <small>dài</small>

3　A Little Dilemma　有 点 儿 矛 盾

成　(v + 成) **become, into**　When used after a verb, 成 leads to a change.

他决定把头发染成紫色的。 <small>rǎn　zǐ</small>

我把蛋糕切成八块，分给所有的人。 <small>dàn　qiē</small>

她把长裤剪成短裤，看起来还挺不错的。 <small>kù jiǎn</small>

老师昨天把我看成你了。

禁不起　**unable to resist, unable to endure**

她禁不起店员的怂恿，买了很多名牌衣服。 <small>jīn　yuán　sǒng yǒng</small>

他禁不起同学的怂恿，也跟着抽烟了。 <small>sǒng yǒng</small>

我禁不起热，一回家就跳到游泳池里。 <small>tiào　chí</small>

怪怪的　**odd, weird, strange**

我戴上了肚脐环后感觉怪怪的。 <small>dài　qí</small>

那道菜吃起来怪怪的。

他今天看起来怪怪的。

今天天气怪怪的。

究竟[jiūjìng]　**actually, the very end**

你究竟是去还是不去，应该做个决定。 <small>yīng</small>

告诉我，你究竟喜欢谁？ <small>gào sù</small>

大家都不知道她究竟在想什么。

你究竟有没有钱？

矛盾　[máodùn] **contradictory, having contradicting thoughts, be in a dilemma**

究竟要不要跟男朋友分手，她的心里也很矛盾。

去不去英国上大学，我也很矛盾。

你听过"自相矛盾"这个成语故事吗？

4　Unpleasant Happenings　不愉快的事

自从　**since, ever since**　It indicates a starting point in the past and is commonly

followed by 以后.

自从我们吵架以后，我一直没见过他。

自从开始打工以后，我每天都很累。

自从你走了以后，我天天想你。

接　　(1) **receive (letter, message), answer (telephone)**

我昨天接到五封信。

我接到了爸爸发回来的传真。

我打电话给她，可是她不接。

(2) **meet, pick up (someone)**

我明天下午三点来接你。

我们去机场接陈老师。

向……问好　**send regards to...; say hello to...**

请代我向大家问好。

请代我向你爸爸、妈妈问好。

叔叔来了，我去向他问好。

4

生　词

1　Not a Big Deal　没什么大不了

大不了	dàbuliǎo	*colloq.* serious, big deal (没什么大不了 - no big deal)
吓……一跳	xià...yí tiào	*v.* startle (someone) 吓 - to scare, to frighten; 跳 - jump, to jump
发呆	fādāi	*v.* be lost in thought, stare blankly 发 - to happen, to send; 呆 - stupid
页	yè	*n.* page
小生	xiǎoshēng	*n.* young man (a role in Chinese opera)
提	tí	*v.* mention; carry (e.g. a bucket)
吹了	chuī le	*colloq.* broke up (with girlfriend or boyfriend) 吹 - to blow
个性	gèxìng	*n.* personality 个 - individual; 性 - nature, character

分手	fēnshǒu	*v.* break up, part company 分- to part; 手- hand
个子	gèzi	*n.* height, stature build
帅	shuài	*adj.* handsome, good-looking
出风头	chūfēngtou	*v.* be in the spotlight, be very popular; show off 出- to come out; 风头- public attention
孩子	háizi	*n.* child 女孩子- girl; 男孩子- boy
心目中	xīnmùzhōng	*phr.* in one's eyes 心- heart; 目- eye; 中- in, middle, centre
白马王子	báimǎ-wángzǐ	*n.* prince charming 白马- white horse; 王子- prince
崇拜	chóngbài	*v.* adore, worship 崇- to adore, to worship; 拜- to worship
骄傲	jiāo'ào	*adj.* arrogant, conceited 骄- arrogant; 傲- arrogant
难过	nánguò	*adj.* sad 难- difficult; 过- to pass
哈	hā	(sound of laughter) hah
可……了	kě...le	*colloq.* absolutely, really (used for emphasis)
赞成	zànchéng	*v.* approve of, agree with (oppose, be against- 反对) 赞- to support; 成- to become, to succeed
认为	rènwéi	*v.* think that..., consider that...
开通	kāitōng	*adj.* open-minded, liberal 开- to open; 通- through, to get through
道理	dàoli	*n.* truth, argument 道- way, road; 理- reason, logic
毕业	bìyè	*v.* graduate 毕- to finish; 业- course of study
将来	jiānglái	*n.* future 将- to be going to; 来- to come
进入	jìnrù	*v.* enter 进- to enter; 入- to enter
白日梦	báirìmèng	*n.* day dream 白日- day; 梦- dream
迷人	mírén	*adj.* charming 迷- to charm; 人- person, people
壮	zhuàng	*adj.* strong, muscular
聪明	cōngming	*adj.* intelligent, bright, clever 聪- clever; 明- bright
看法	kànfǎ	*n.* viewpoint, opinion 看- to think, to see; 法- way, method
离开	líkāi	*v.* leave 离- to leave; 开- away, to open, to begin
永远	yǒngyuǎn	*adv.* forever 永- always, forever; 远- far
养老院	yǎnglǎoyuàn	*n.* retirement village 养- to raise; 老- old, elderly; 院- yard

2 Just for Fun 好玩而已

而已	éryǐ	*part.* that's all, nothing more
身上	shēnshàng	*n.* on one's body 身- body; 上- on
说谎	shuōhuǎng	*v.* lie 说- to tell, to speak; 谎- lie
明明	míngmíng	*adv.* clearly, obviously
闻	wén	*v.* smell
老实说来	lǎoshí shuō lái	*v.* speak out honestly 老实- honestly, honest
抽	chōu	*v.* smoke (cigarette, pipe); to take out, to draw
根	gēn	*m.w.* for long and thin objects (e.g. cigarette)
规定	guīdìng	*v.* stipulate; *n.* rule, regulation 规- to regulate; 定- to decide
准	zhǔn	*v.* allow
香烟	xiāngyān	*n.* cigarette 香- fragrant; 烟- cigarette, smoke
身体	shēntǐ	*n.* body 身- body; 体- body
有害	yǒuhài	*adj.* harmful 对……有害- to be harmful to...; 害- harm
上瘾	shàngyǐn	*v.* be addicted to 上- to go to; 瘾- addiction
麻烦	máfan	*adj.* troublesome; *n. & v.* trouble

4

生词

吸毒	xīdú	v. do drugs 吸- to inhale, to suck; 毒- poison, poisonous, to poison
过量	guòliàng	adj. overdose 过- to pass; 量- quantity
死掉	sǐdiào	v. die 死- to die, death; 掉- [a particle]; away, out
两回事	liǎng huí shì	n. two different matters 回- m.w. for matter; 事- matter, affair
干吗	gànmá	colloq. why on earth; whatever for
扯	chě	v. pull, drag
戒烟	jièyān	v. quit smoking 戒- to quit; 烟- cigarette, smoke
说是这么说	shuō shì zhème shuō	colloq. so you say
一旦	yídàn	adv. once, in case, now that
戒	jiè	v. quit, give up 戒得掉- able to quit; 戒不掉- unable to quit
毛病	máobìng	n. fault, mistake 毛- hair; 病- illness, sick
犯	fàn	v. commit (a fault, a mistake, a crime)
反正	fǎnzheng	adv. anyway, anyhow, in any case 反- reverse; 正- obverse
在于	zài yú	v. be determined by, depend on
小题大做	xiǎotí-dàzuò	idiom make a mountain out of a molehill
忘掉	wàngdiào	v. forget 忘- to forget; 掉- [a particle;, away, out
派头	pàitóu	n. style, manner, panache
犯罪	fànzuì	v. commit a crime 犯- to commit; 罪- crime
惹	rě	v. provoke, ask for something undesirable
结果	jiéguǒ	adv. as a result, in the end; n. result 结- to conclude; 果- fruit
非吸烟区	fēi xīyān qū	n. non-smoking area

3　A Little Dilemma　有点儿矛盾

矛盾	máodùn	adj. contradictory, having contradicting thoughts, be in a dilemma 矛- spear; 盾- shield
提议	tíyì	v. suggest 提- to bring up; 议- opinion, view
染	rǎn	v. dye
美容院	měiróngyuàn	n. beauty salon 美- to beautify, beautiful; 容- appearance; 院- yard
边	biān	n. side; suffix of a noun of locality, e.g. 右边- right; 左边- left; 东边- east; 西边- west
特别	tèbié	adj. special 特- special; 别- n. distinction, v. don't
穿	chuān	v. pierce, penetrate; wear, put on
肚脐洞	dùqídòng	n. navel piercing 肚脐- navel; 洞- hole
禁不起	jīnbuqǐ	v. be unable to resist, be unable to endure
跟	gēn	v. follow or accompany; conj. and, with; prep. towards, with
肚脐	dùqí	n. navel
戴	dài	v. wear (hat, glasses, ring, etc.)
环	huán	n. ring, hoop
心里	xīnli	in (one's) heart
怪怪的	guàiguàide	adj. odd, strange, weird
究竟	jiūjìng	adv. actually, the very end 究- after all; 竟- to complete, eventually
作怪	zuòguài	v. act mischievously, create mischief 作- to do, to make; 怪- odd, strange
偷偷地	tōutōude	adv. stealthily, secretly 偷- to steal
赶	gǎn	v. pursue, catch up with

4

新潮	xīncháo	*n.* new trend; *adj.* trendy, fashionable　新- new; 潮- wave, tide
坏事	huàishì	*n.* bad thing, evil deed　坏- bad; 事- matter, affair
打扮	dǎbàn	*n.* style of dress; *v.* dress up　打- to hit; 扮- to be dressed up as
保守	bǎoshǒu	*adj.* conservative　保- to keep; 守- to abide by, to observe
开明	kāimíng	*adj.* open-minded, enlightened　开- to open; 明- to understand
说不定	shuōbudìng	*adv.* perhaps, maybe
文身	wénshēn	*v & n.* tatoo　文- to tattoo, lines; 身- body
抱怨	bàoyuàn	*v.* complain　抱- to hug, to embrace; 怨- resentment, to blame
老古板	lǎogǔbǎn	*n.* old fogey
减肥	jiǎnféi	*v.* lose weight　减- to reduce, to subtract; 肥- fat
自相矛盾	zìxiāng-máodùn	*idiom* be self-contradictory　自- self; 相- mutual　矛盾- contradictory
矛	máo	*n.* spear
刺	cì	*v.* poke
任何	rènhé	*adj.* any, whatever
盾	dùn	*n.* shield
成语	chéngyǔ	*n.* idiom

4　Unpleasant Happenings　不 愉 快 的 事

自从	zìcóng	*prep.* since, ever since　自- since; 从- from
接	jiē	*v.* receive (message); meet, pick up (someone)
贴	tiē	*v.* paste
碰	pèng	*v.* encounter
另	lìng	*adj. & adv.* another
撞上	zhuàngshang	*v.* run into, strike
陈英	Chén Yīng	*n.* a Chinese name
插队	chāduì	*v.* cut into a queue　插- to insert; 队- queue
结果	jiéguǒ	*adv.* as a result, in the end; *n.* result　结- to conclude; 果- fruit
轮	lún	*v.* take turns
气人	qìrén	*adj.* annoying　气- to enrage, to annoy; 人- person, people
你说气不气人？ Nǐ shuō qì bú qìrén? *colloq.* Don't you think it's annoying?
吓坏了	xià huài le	*colloq.* be terribly scared
参考书	cānkǎoshū	*n.* reference book used to complement the textbook　参考- to refer
用功	yònggōng	*adj.* diligent, hard-working　用- to use; 功- effort, merit
发现	fāxiàn	*v.* discover
专心	zhuānxīn	*v.* concentrate; *adj.* attentive, absorbed　专- to engross; 心- heart
重要	zhòngyào	*adj.* important　重- heavy
代	dài	*v.* act on behalf of others
问好	wènhǎo	*v.* send one's regards, say hello　问- to ask; 好- good, well
课文	kèwén	*n.* text　课- lesson; 文- writing
背	bèi	*v.* memorize, learn by heart
打	dǎ	*v.* guess [special use for riddle hints]
物	wù	*n.* object, thing
同意	tóngyì	*v.* consent, agree, approve　同- the same; 意- idea, meaning
词	cí	*n.* word, term

学写字

页 yè *page*	别 bié *don't; distinction; other*	吹 chuī *to blow*	性 xìng *character, nature*	吵 chǎo *to quarrel; noisy*
架 jià *shelf, rack*	难 nán *difficult*	赞 zàn *to support*	其 qí *that, such*	实 shí *truth*
抽 chōu *to smoke, to draw*	身 shēn *body*	体 tǐ *body*	害 hài *harm*	报 bào *to report; newspaper*
纸 zhǐ *paper*	消 xiāo *to vanish*	容 róng *to hold; appearance*	易 yì *easy*	题 tí *topic; question*
逛 guàng *to stroll*	特 tè *special*	怪 guài *odd, strange*	轻 qīng *light (in weight)*	更 gèng *even, more*
种 zhǒng *kind, type, sort*	奇 qí *unusual*	接 jiē *to pick up, to receive*	愉 yú *happy, pleased*	被 bèi *[passive signifier]*
队 duì *team, queue*	应 yīng; yìng *should; to adapt*	结 jié *to conclude*	功 gōng *merit, effort*	绩 jī *result*

4

Appendix 1

WORDS AND EXPRESSIONS
Chinese-English

Simplified	Pinyin	English	Traditional	Lesson
A 阿德莱德	Ādéláidé	*n.* Adelaide [transliteration]	阿德萊德	2-4
艾尔岩	Ài'ěryán	*n.* Ayers Rock (Uluru)	艾爾岩	2-4
安排	ānpái	*v.* arrange	安排	3-1
桉树	ānshù	*n.* eucalyptus tree	桉樹	2-4
B 把	bǎ	grammatical word, see p. 41	把	2-1
白马王子	báimǎ-wángzǐ	*n.* prince charming	白馬王子	4-1
白日梦	báirìmèng	*n.* day dream	白日夢	4-1
摆	bǎi	*v.* set up, arrange, place	擺	1-3
班会	bānhuì	*n.* class meeting	班會	1-2
班上	bānshàng	in the class	班上	1-3
班长	bānzhǎng	*n.* class leader	班長	1-2
班主任	bānzhǔrèn	*n.* form teacher	班主任	1-2
帮忙	bāngmáng	*adj.* helpful; *v.* help	幫忙	2-4
傍晚	bàngwǎn	*n.* dusk, early evening	傍晚	2-4
保护	bǎohù	*v.* protect; *n.* protection	保護	2-4
保龄球	bǎolíngqiú	*n.* bowling [transliteration]	保齡球	3-1
保姆	bǎomǔ	*n.* baby-sitter, nanny	保姆	3-1
保守	bǎoshǒu	*adj.* conservative	保守	4-3
报告	bàogào	*n.* report	報告	1-4
抱怨	bàoyuàn	*v.* complain	抱怨	4-3
北海公园	Běihǎi Gōngyuán	*n.* Beihai Park	北海公園	1-1
被	bèi	passive signifier, see p. 68	被	3-4
背	bèi	*n.* memorize, learn by heart	背	4-4
笨	bèn	*adj.* stupid	笨	2-3
比萨饼	bǐsàbǐng	*n.* pizza [transliteration]	比薩餅	2-2
敝	bì	*pron.* a humble form of *my* or *our*	敝	1-2
毕业	bìyè	*v.* graduate	畢業	4-1
边	biān	*n.* side; suffix of a noun of locality	邊	4-3
便餐	biàncān	*n.* simple meal	便餐	2-3
表现	biǎoxiàn	*v.* behave; *n.* behaviour	表現	2-4
别人	biérén	*n.* other people	別人	3-3
并(不)	bìng(bù)	*adv.* (not) at all [used before a negative word for emphasis]	并(不)	2-4
不但……而且	búdàn... érqiě	*conj.* not only... but also	不但……而且	3-2
不得了	bùdéliǎo	*adv.* extremely, exceedingly	不得了	2-1
不可开交	bù kě kāi jiāo	*adv.* awfully, terribly	不可開交	1-3
不可思议	bù kě sīyì	*adj.* unbelievable, beyond one's imagination	不可思議	2-1
不停地	bù tíng de	*adv.* continuously, frequently	不停地	2-1
不准	bùzhǔn	*v.* not allow, forbid	不准	1-4

Simplified	Pinyin	English	Traditional	Lesson
C 擦	cā	*v.* apply, rub, put on	擦	1-1
才	cái	*adv.* just, only just	才	1-1
餐	cān	*n.* meal	餐	3-4
餐馆	cānguǎn	*n.* restaurant	餐館	3-2
餐厅	cāntīng	*n.* restaurant	餐廳	2-3
参考书	cānkǎoshū	*n.* reference book used to complement the textbook	參考書	4-4
藏	cáng	*v.* hide	藏	3-2
曾经	céngjīng	*adv.* once, formerly, ever	曾經	3-2
插队	chāduì	*v.* cut into a queue	插隊	4-4
差	chà	*adj.* poor, not up to standard; *v.* differ (by), be short	差	2-1, 3-2
唱片行	chàngpiànháng	*n.* music store	唱片行	3-1
吵	chǎo	*adj.* noisy; *v.* disturb, quarrel	吵	3-3
炒面	chǎomiàn	*n.* fried noodle	炒麵	2-2
车箱	chēxiāng	*n.* trunk, boot (of car)	車箱	2-3
扯	chě	*v.* pull, drag	扯	4-2
陈英	Chén Yīng	*n.* a Chinese name	陳英	4-4
成绩	chéngjī	*n.* achievement, result	成績	3-4
成为	chéngwéi	*v.* become	成為	1-1
成语	chéngyǔ	*n.* idiom	成語	4-3
崇拜	chóngbài	*v.* adore, worship	崇拜	4-1
抽	chōu	*v.* smoke (cigarette, pipe), take out, draw	抽	4-2
筹备	chóubèi	*v.* arrange, prepare	籌備	1-3
出风头	chūfēngtou	*v.* be in the spotlight, be very popular	出風頭	4-1
除了…以外	chúle...yǐwài	*prep.* besides, apart from, in addition to; except	除了…以外	1-3
穿	chuān	*v.* pierce, penetrate; wear, put on	穿	4-3
传真	chuánzhēn	*n.* facsimile	傳真	1-4
传真机	chuánzhēnjī	*n.* fax machine	傳真機	1-4
吹了	chuī le	*colloq.* broke up (with girlfriend or boyfriend)	吹了	4-1
词	cí	*n.* word, term	詞	4-4
辞掉	cídiào	*v.* quit, resign, sack	辭掉	3-2
刺	cì	*v.* poke	刺	4-3
聪明	cōngming	*adj.* intelligent, bright, clever	聰明	4-1
从	cóng	*adv.* since, from	從	3-3
存	cún	*v.* save, deposit	存	3-3
D 打	dǎ	*v.* guess [special use for riddle hints]	打	4-4
打扮	dǎbàn	*n.* style of dress; *v.* dress up	打扮	4-3
打工	dǎgōng	*v.* have a part-time job	打工	3-1
打瞌睡	dǎ kēshuì	*v.* doze off	打瞌睡	2-4
大堡礁	Dàbǎojiāo	*n.* Great Barrier Reef	大堡礁	2-4
大部分	dàbùfen	*n.* most	大部分	1-3
大不了	dàbuliǎo	*colloq.* serious, big deal	大不了	4-1
代	dài	*v.* act on behalf of others	代	4-4
戴	dài	*v.* wear (hat, glasses, ring, etc.)	戴	4-3
带路	dàilù	*v.* lead the way	帶路	1-1
袋鼠	dàishǔ	*n.* kangaroo	袋鼠	2-4
担心	dānxīn	*v.* worry	擔心	1-2
当	dāng	*v.* be, work as, serve as, e.g. 当爸爸, 当班长	當	1-2

Simplified	Pinyin	English	Traditional	Lesson
当时	dāngshí	*adv.* at that time, then	當時	3-1
捣蛋	dǎodàn	*v.* make trouble	搗蛋	2-4
到处	dàochù	*adv.* everywhere	到處	3-2
到底	dàodǐ	*adv.* [in a question] after all, on earth, really	到底	1-2
道理	dàoli	*n.* truth, argument	道理	4-1
道歉	dàoqiàn	*v.* apologize	道歉	1-4
道谢	dàoxiè	*v.* express one's gratitude, thank	道謝	1-1
等	děng	*pron.* and so on, and so forth; *v.* wait	等	2-2
地方	dìfāng	*adj.* local; *n.* place, location	地方	3-1
底下	dǐxia	*prep.* under, beneath	底下	1-1
电	diàn	*n.* electricity	電	2-4
电影世界	Diànyǐng Shìjiè	*n.* Movie World	電影世界	1-1
电子邮件	diànzǐ yóujiàn	*n.* e-mail	電子郵件	1-4
电子游戏	diànzǐ yóuxì	*n.* computer games	電子遊戲	1-4
电子邮址	diànzǐ yóuzhǐ	*n.* e-mail address	電子郵址	1-4
店员	diànyuán	*n.* clerk, salesperson	店員	3-1
鼎鼎大名	dǐngdǐng dàmíng	*adj.* well-known, famous, celebrated	鼎鼎大名	2-4
丢	diū	*v.* throw, lose	丢	2-3
丢掉	diūdiào	*v.* throw away	丢掉	3-2
丢人	diūrén	*colloq.* embarrassing; *v.* lose face	丢人	2-3
动心	dòngxīn	*adj.* heart set on (something or someone)	動心	3-3
豆浆	dòujiāng	*n.* soya milk	豆漿	2-2
肚脐	dùqí	*n.* navel	肚臍	4-3
肚脐洞	dùqídòng	*n.* navel piercing	肚臍洞	4-3
对……来说	duì...lái shuō	as for...	對……來說	3-4
对联	duìlián	*n.* a Chinese couplet written on scrolls etc.	對聯	2-4
盾	dùn	*n.* shield	盾	4-3
炖羊肉	dùnyángròu	*n.* lamb stew	燉羊肉	2-2
多半	duōbàn	*adv.* mostly	多半	1-1
E 而且	érqiě	*conj.* also, moreover, in addition	而且	3-2
而已	éryǐ	*part.* that's all, nothing more	而已	4-2
二手烟	èrshǒuyān	*n.* passive smoking	二手煙	3-2
F 发	fā	*v.* send (e.g. email, fax); discover;	發	1-4
	fà	*n.* hair	髮	
发呆	fādāi	*v.* be lost in thought, stare blankly	發呆	4-1
发脾气	fā píqi	*v.* lose temper	發脾氣	3-2
发现	fāxiàn	*v.* discover	發現	4-4
翻	fān	*v.* turn over	翻	2-1
反正	fǎnzhèng	*adv.* anyway, anyhow, in any case	反正	1-2, 4-2
犯	fàn	*v.* commit (a fault, a mistake, a crime)	犯	4-2
犯罪	fànzuì	*v.* commit a crime	犯罪	4-2
方便	fāngbiàn	*adj.* convenient	方便	1-4
方式	fāngshì	*n.* way	方式	3-1
房间	fángjiān	*n.* room	房間	2-1
防晒霜	fángshàishuāng	*n.* sunscreen	防曬霜	1-1
放假	fàngjià	*v.* have a holiday or vacation	放假	1-1

Simplified	Pinyin	English	Traditional	Lesson
放心	fàngxīn	*v.* stop worrying, be at ease	放心	1-2
非吸烟区	fēi xīyān qū	*n.* non-smoking area	非吸煙區	4-2
废品	fèipǐn	*n.* junk, waste	廢品	2-3
分手	fēnshǒu	*v.* break up, part company	分手	4-1
丰富	fēngfù	*adj.* diverse and plentiful	豐富	2-2
风景	fēngjǐng	*n.* scenery	風景	2-1
服饰店	fúshìdiàn	*n.* fashion shop	服飾店	3-1, 3-3
服务员	fúwùyuán	*n.* waiter, waitress	服務員	3-1
付	fù	*v.* pay	付	3-2
副	fù	*m.w.* pair	副	2-4
父母亲	fùmǔqīn	*n.* parents	父母親	2-1
G 咖喱	gālí	*n.* curry [transliteration]	咖喱	2-2
干杯	gānbēi	*colloq.* bottoms up	乾杯	3-4
赶	gǎn	*v.* pursue, catch up with	趕	4-3
感觉	gǎnjué	*n.* feeling; *v.* feel	感覺	3-1
干吗	gànmá	*colloq.* why on earth; whatever for	幹麼	4-2
高尔夫球	gāo'ěrfūqiú	*n.* golf [transliteration]	高爾夫球	1-3
歌剧院	gējùyuàn	*n.* opera house	歌劇院	2-4
各处	gèchù	*adv.* every place	各處	2-4
各国	gèguó	*n.* every country	各國	2-2
各自	gèzì	*adv.* respectively	各自	3-3
个性	gèxìng	*n.* personality	個性	4-1
个子	gèzi	*n.* height, stature build	個子	4-1
跟	gēn	*prep.* towards or with; *conj.* and; *v.* follow or accompany	跟	3-1, 4-3
根	gēn	*m.w.* for long and thin objects (e.g. cigarette)	根	4-2
弓	gōng	*n.* bow	弓	1-2
功能	gōngnéng	*n.* function	功能	1-4
工资	gōngzī	*n.* salary, wage	工資	3-1
恭喜	gōngxǐ	*v.* congratulate; *n.* congratulations	恭喜	1-2
谷类食物	gǔ lèi shíwù	*n.* cereal	穀類食物	2-2
顾客	gùkè	*n.* customer, client	顧客	3-2
怪怪的	guàiguàide	*adj.* odd, strange, weird	怪怪的	4-3
关心	guānxīn	*v.* care about	關心	1-2
关系	guānxì	*n.* relation, relationship	關係	1-2
罐子	guànzi	*n.* tin, can, jar, jug	罐子	2-3
光盘	guāngpán	*n.* CD Rom	光盤	1-4
光阴似箭	guāngyīn sì jiàn	*idiom* time flies	光陰似箭	1-1
广告	guǎnggào	*n.* advertisement	廣告	3-1
规定	guīdìng	*v.* stipulate; *n.* rule, regulation	規定	4-2
贵	guì	a respectful form of *your*	貴	1-2
国际	guójì	*adj.* international	國際	2-4
国际象棋	guójì xiàngqí	*n.* chess	國際象棋	1-3
国王	guówáng	*n.* king	國王	1-2
过来	guòlái	(1) *v.* come over; (2) grammatical term, see p. 18	過來	1-2
过量	guòliàng	*adj.* overdose	過量	4-2
过意不去	guòyì bú qù	*v.* feel guilty about	過意不去	3-1

Simplified	Pinyin	English	Traditional	Lesson
H 哈	hā	(sound of laughter) hah	哈	4-1
孩子	háizi	*n.* child	孩子	4-1
海边	hǎibiān	*n.* seashore, seaside, beach	海邊	1-1
海鲜	hǎixiān	*n.* seafood	海鮮	2-2
海洋世界	Hǎiyáng Shìjiè	*n.* Sea World	海洋世界	1-1
耗电	hàodiàn	*v.* consume a lot of electricity	耗電	2-4
喝酒	hē jiǔ	*v.* drink wine/liquor	喝酒	3-2
合唱团	héchàngtuán	*n.* choir	合唱團	1-3
红茶	hóngchá	*n.* black tea	紅茶	2-2
红通通	hóngtōngtōng	*adj.* red through and through	紅通通	1-1
糊涂虫	hútuchóng	*n.* blunderer, bungler	糊塗蟲	1-2
互相	hùxiāng	*adv.* mutually, each other	互相	1-4
花	huā	*v.* spend, e.g. 花钱 - spend moeny; *n.* flower	花	3-1
划船	huáchuán	*n.* rowing; *v.* row a boat	划船	1-3
划算	huásuàn	*adj.* worth the cost	划算	3-4
坏处	huàichù	*n.* drawback, disadvantage	壞處	3-4, 4-2
坏事	huàishì	*n.* bad thing, evil deed	壞事	4-3
环	huán	*n.* ring, hoop; *v.* to surround	環	4-3
环境	huánjìng	*n.* environment	環境	2-4, 3-2
换	huàn	*v.* change, exchange	換	3-1
回报	huíbào	*n.* return, reward	回報	3-1
回收	huíshōu	*v.* recycle	回收	2-3
回头	huítóu	*v.* turn one's head, turn around	回頭	2-4
活动	huódòng	*n.* activity	活動	1-2
火锅	huǒguō	*n.* hot pot	火鍋	2-3
J 几乎	jīhū	*adv.* almost	幾乎	2-4
继续	jìxù	*v.* continue	繼續	2-3
佳	jiā	*adj.* good, fine, beautiful	佳	1-2
加	jiā	*v.* add	加	2-2
加入	jiārù	*v.* join in	加入	1-3
加温	jiāwēn	*v.* heat	加溫	2-4
假期	jiàqī	*n.* vacation	假期	1-1
价钱	jiàqián	*n.* price	價錢	3-3
煎蛋	jiāndàn	*n.* fried egg	煎蛋	2-2
减肥	jiǎnféi	*v.* lose weight	減肥	4-3
饯行	jiànxíng	*v.* give a farewell party	餞行	3-4
将来	jiānglái	*n.* future	將來	4-1
讲话	jiǎnghuà	*v.* talk, speak	講話	2-1
奖学金	jiǎngxuéjīn	*n.* scholarship	獎學金	3-4
交	jiāo	*v.* pay (a fee, tuition)	交	3-1
交换	jiāohuàn	*v.* exchange, swap	交換	1-1
交朋友	jiāo péngyou	*v.* make friends	交朋友	1-1
骄傲	jiāo'ào	*adj.* arrogant, conceited	驕傲	4-1
接	jiē	*v.* receive (message); meet, pick up (someone)	接	4-4
结果	jiéguǒ	*adv.* as a result, in the end; *n.* result	結果	4-2, 4-4
戒	jiè	*v.* quit, give up	戒	4-2

Simplified	Pinyin	English	Traditional	Lesson
戒烟	jièyān	*v.* quit smoking	戒煙	4-2
禁不起	jīnbuqǐ	*v.* be unable to resist, be unable to endure	禁不起	4-3
进入	jìnrù	*v.* enter	進入	4-1
经过	jīngguò	*v.* go past	經過	2-1
经验	jīngyàn	*n.* experience	經驗	3-1
惊讶	jīngyà	*adj.* surprised	驚訝	3-4
敬	jìng	*v.* propose a toast, offer politely	敬	3-4
究竟	jiūjìng	*adv.* actually, the very end	究竟	4-3
酒馆	jiǔguǎn	*n.* bar, pub	酒館	3-2
聚餐	jùcān	*n.* dinner party; *v.* have a dinner party	聚餐	2-3, 3-4
据说	jùshuō	it is said, allegedly	據說	2-4
决定	juédìng	*v.* decide	決定	2-1
K 咖啡	kāfēi	*n.* coffee	咖啡	2-2
咖啡馆	kāfēiguǎn	*n.* coffee shop	咖啡館	2-3, 3-1
开	kāi	*v.* (1) hold, operate; (2) start, open	開	1-2
开明	kāimíng	*adj.* open-minded, enlightened	開明	4-3
开通	kāitōng	*adj.* open-minded, liberal	開通	4-1
开心	kāixīn	*v.* feel happy, rejoice	開心	1-1
开学	kāixué	*v.* school starts	開學	1-1
堪培拉	Kānpéilā	*n.* Canberra [transliteration]	堪培拉	2-4
看法	kànfǎ	*n.* viewpoint, opinion	看法	4-1
烤	kǎo	*v.* toast, bake, roast, grill	烤	2-2
烤鸡	kǎojī	*n.* barbecue chicken	烤雞	2-2
烤肉	kǎoròu	*v. & n.* barbecue	烤肉	2-3
烤肉饼	kǎoròubǐng	*n.* meat pie	烤肉餅	2-2
考拉	kǎolā	*n.* koala, called 无尾熊 wúwěixióng in Taiwan	考拉	2-4
可……了	kě...le	*colloq.* absolutely, really (emphasis)	可……了	4-1
可惜	kěxī	it's a pity, too bad	可惜	3-2
课文	kèwén	*n.* text	課文	4-4
肯	kěn	*v.* be willing to	肯	3-1
空	kōng	*adj.* empty; *n.* [kòng] free time	空	2-3
空气	kōngqì	*n.* air	空氣	2-1
空手道	kōngshǒudào	*n.* karate	空手道	1-3
孔子	Kǒngzǐ	*n.* Confucius (551 BC – 479 BC), Chinese philosopher	孔子	2-1
酷	kù	*slang* cool [transliteration]; cruel, extreme	酷	3-3
快餐店	kuàicāndiàn	*n.* fast-food restaurant	快餐店	3-1
L 垃圾	lājī	*n.* rubbish, garbage	垃圾	2-3
辣	là	*adj.* hot (of taste)	辣	2-2
浪费	làngfèi	*v.* waste; *adj.* wasteful	浪費	1-4
唠叨	láodāo	*v.* nag	嘮叨	3-3
老板	lǎobǎn	*n.* boss	老闆	3-2
老古板	lǎogǔbǎn	*n.* old fogey	老古板	4-3
老实说来	lǎoshí shuō lái	*v.* speak out honestly	老實說來	4-2
老是	lǎoshì	*adv.* always, all the time	老是	3-1
垒球	lěiqiú	*n.* softball	壘球	1-3
离开	líkāi	*v.* leave	離開	4-1

Simplified	Pinyin	English	Traditional	Lesson
立	lì	*v.* stand	立	1-2
例句	lìjù	*n.* example sentence	例句	1-1
利用	lìyòng	*v.* use, make use of	利用	1-4
联系	liánxì	*v.* contact, get in touch with	聯繫	1-4
练	liàn	*v.* practise	練	1-3
练习	liànxí	*n.* exercise, practice	練習	1-3
两回事	liǎng huí shì	*n.* two different matters	兩回事	4-2
聊	liáo	*v.* chat	聊	1-1
聊天儿	liáotiānr	*v.* chat	聊天兒	1-1
聊天室	liáotiān shì	*n.* chat room	聊天室	1-4
了解	liǎojiě	*v.* understand; *n.* understanding	瞭解	1-1
料子	liàozi	*n.* material (fabric)	料子	3-3
临时	línshí	*adv.* at the time (when something happens)	臨時	3-1
零花	línghuā	*v.* spend pocket money	零花	3-3
零花钱	línghuāqián	*n.* pocket money	零花錢	3-1
领	lǐng	*v.* get, receive (money or prize)	領	3-1
另	lìng	*adj. & adv.* another	另	4-4
流利	liúlì	*adj.* fluent	流利	3-4
流行	liúxíng	*adj.* popular, in fashion	流行	3-1
路过	lùguò	*v.* pass by	路過	2-2
陆续	lùxù	*adv.* one after another	陸續	2-3
露营	lùyíng	*v.* camp; *n.* camping	露營	1-1
乱	luàn	*adj.* messy	亂	3-2
轮	lún	*v.* take turns	輪	4-4
论语	Lúnyǔ	*n.* 'The Analects of Confucius'	論語	2-1
吕	Lǚ	*n.* a surname	呂	1-2
旅馆	lǚguǎn	*n.* hotel	旅館	1-1
M 麻烦	máfan	*adj.* troublesome; *n. & v.* trouble	麻煩	4-2
骂	mà	*v.* scold, condemn	罵	1-4
麦片粥	màipiànzhōu	*n.* oatmeal porridge	麥片粥	2-2
矛	máo	*n.* spear	矛	4-3
矛盾	máodùn	*adj.* contradictory, having contradicting thoughts, be in a dilemma	矛盾	4-3
馒头	mántou	*n.* plain steamed bun	饅頭	2-2
毛病	máobìng	*n.* fault, mistake	毛病	4-2
没什么大不了	méi shénme dàbuliǎo	*colloq.* no big deal	沒什麼大不了	4-1
美容院	měiróngyuàn	*n.* beauty salon	美容院	4-3
迷人	mírén	*adj.* charming	迷人	4-1
面条	miàntiáo	*n.* noodles	麵條	2-2
明明	míngmíng	*adv.* clearly, obviously	明明	2-3, 4-2
名牌	míngpái	*n.* famous brand	名牌	3-3
木	mù	*n.* tree, wood	木	1-2
N 难过	nánguò	*adj.* sad	難過	4-1
难免	nánmiǎn	*adj.* inevitable, unavoidable	難免	3-1
闹事	nàoshì	*v.* make trouble, create a disturbance	鬧事	3-2
内向	nèixiàng	*adj.* introvert	內向	1-2

Simplified	Pinyin	English	Traditional	Lesson
能够	nénggòu	*aux.* can, be capable of	能夠	2-2
你说气不气人?		*colloq.* Don't you think it's annoying?	你說氣不氣人?	4-4
	Nǐ shuō qì bú qìrén			

P 怕	pà	*v.* be afraid of	怕	2-1
排球	páiqiú	*n.* volleyball	排球	1-3
派头	pàitóu	*n.* style, manner, panache	派頭	4-2
盘子	pánzi	*n.* plate	盤子	2-3
泡	pào	*v.* brew (tea or coffee), soak	泡	2-2
碰	pèng	*v.* encounter	碰	4-4
啤酒	píjiǔ	*n.* beer	啤酒	2-3
脾气	píqi	*n.* temper	脾氣	3-2
瓶子	píngzi	*n.* bottle, jar	瓶子	2-3
珀斯	Pòsī	*n.* Perth [transliteration]	珀斯	2-4

Q 妻子	qīzi	*n.* wife	妻子	2-4
其他	qítā	*pron.* other, others	其他	2-2
起来	qǐlai	*suffix,* see p. 66	起來	3-2
气人	qìrén	*adj.* annoying	氣人	4-4
请上坐	qǐng shàngzuò	please have the best seat	請上坐	2-4
区	qū	*n.* area, district	區	2-3
全国	quánguó	*adj.* national; *n.* entire country	全國	1-3
全身	quánshēn	*n.* entire body	全身	1-1

R 然后	ránhòu	*adv.* afterwards, then	然後	2-1
染	rǎn	*v.* dye	染	4-3
饶	ráo	*v.* have mercy on	饒	1-2
惹	rě	*v.* provoke, ask for something undesirable	惹	4-2
热闹	rènào	*adj.* bustling with noise and excitement	熱鬧	2-1
热情	rèqíng	*adj.* warm, hospitable, enthusiastic	熱情	2-4
热心	rèxīn	*adj.* enthusiastic	熱心	1-1
人	rén	*n.* personality, e.g. 人很好; personal feature, e.g. 人很高	人	3-2
人行横道	rénxíng héngdào	*n.* pedestrian crossing	人行橫道	2-1
人选	rénxuǎn	*n.* candidate	人選	1-2
人缘儿	rényuánr	*n.* relations with people; popularity	人緣兒	1-2
任何	rènhé	*adj.* any, whatever	任何	4-3
任你吃到饱	rèn nǐ chī dào bǎo	*phr.* all you can eat	任你吃到飽	3-4
认识	rènshi	*v.* know, recognize	認識	2-4
认为	rènwéi	*v.* think that..., consider that...	認為	4-1
认真	rènzhēn	*adj.* conscientious, earnest	認真	1-2
仍然	réngrán	*adv.* still	仍然	2-4
肉串	ròuchuàn	*n.* kebab	肉串	2-3
入乡随俗	rù xiāng suí sú	*idiom* when in Rome, do as the Romans do	入鄉隨俗	2-2

S 散步	sànbù	*v.* take a walk	散步	1-1
沙拉	shālā	*n.* salad [transliteration]	沙拉	2-2, 2-3
晒	shài	*v.* expose to sunlight	曬	1-1

Simplified	Pinyin	English	Traditional	Lesson
上网	shàngwǎng	*v.* get on the internet	上網	1-4
上衣	shàngyī	*n.* upper garment	上衣	3-3
上瘾	shàngyǐn	*v.* be addicted to	上癮	4-2
烧饼	shāobǐng	*n.* baked sesame seed flatcake	燒餅	2-2
设计	shèjì	*v. & n.* design	設計	1-3
申请	shēnqǐng	*v.* apply for	申請	3-4
身上	shēnshàng	*n.* on one's body	身上	4-2
身体	shēntǐ	*n.* body	身體	4-2
什么的	shénmede	*colloq.* and so on, and so forth	什麼的	3-1
生菜	shēngcài	*n.* lettuce, raw vegetable	生菜	2-3
生词	shēngcí	*n.* new word	生詞	1-1
声音	shēngyīn	*n.* sound, voice	聲音	3-3
剩下	shèngxià	*v.* remain, be left	剩下	3-3
实在	shízài	*adv.* really	實在	3-3
试	shì	*v.* try	試	3-2
试穿	shìchuān	*v.* try on (clothes/shoes)	試穿	3-3
适合	shìhé	*v.* suit; *adj.* suitable	適合	3-1
适应	shìyìng	*v.* adapt, get used to	適應	2-2
式样	shìyàng	*n.* style	式樣	3-2, 3-3
收据	shōujù	*n.* receipt	收據	3-2
受	shòu	*v.* receive, bear	受	2-4
受不了	shòu bu liǎo	*colloq.* cannot endure or stand; unbearable	受不了	3-2
蔬菜	shūcài	*n.* vegetable	蔬菜	2-2
舒适	shūshì	*adj.* comfortable, cosy	舒適	2-4
帅	shuài	*adj.* handsome, good-looking	帥	4-1
顺利	shùnlì	*adv.* smoothly, successfully	順利	3-4
说不定	shuōbudìng	*adv.* perhaps, maybe	說不定	4-3
说谎	shuōhuǎng	*v.* lie	說謊	4-2
说是这么说	shuō shì zhème shuō	*colloq.* so you say	說是這麼說	4-2
说一声	shuō yì shēng	*v.* give a word, say (it)	說一聲	1-2
死掉	sǐdiào	*v.* die	死掉	4-2
死机	sǐjī	*v.* break down (computer)	死機	3-2
怂恿	sǒngyǒng	*v.* urge, push, tempt	慫恿	3-3
送报员	sòngbàoyuán	*n.* newsboy	送報員	3-1
宋代	Sòngdài	*n.* Song dynasty (960 - 1279 AD)	宋代	2-4
苏东坡	Sū Dōngpō	*n.* a famous man of letters in Song dynasty	蘇東坡	2-4
塑料袋	sùliàodài	*n.* plastic bag	塑料袋	2-3
随身听	suíshēntīng	*n.* walkman	隨身聽	3-3

T

态度	tàidù	*n.* attitude	態度	3-2
太阳	tàiyáng	*n.* sun	太陽	1-1
太阳镜	tàiyángjìng	*n.* sunglasses	太陽鏡	1-1
太阳能	tàiyángnéng	*n.* solar energy	太陽能	2-4
摊位	tānwèi	*n.* stand, stall	攤位	1-3
谈得来	tán de lái	*v.* get along well, and usually have a good time chatting	談得來	1-1
汤面	tāngmiàn	*n.* noodle soup	湯麵	2-2
糖	táng	*n.* sugar	糖	2-2
讨论	tǎolùn	*v.* discuss; *n.* discussion	討論	1-1

Simplified	Pinyin	English	Traditional	Lesson
特别	tèbié	*adj.* special	特別	4-3
特有	tèyǒu	*adj.* peculiar	特有	2-4
提	tí	*v.* carry (e.g. a luggage); *v.* mention	提	2-1, 4-1
提议	tíyì	*v.* suggest	提議	4-3
体操	tǐcāo	*n.* gymnastics	體操	1-3
贴	tiē	*v.* paste	貼	4-4
通常	tōngcháng	*adv.* usually	通常	1-4
通信	tōngxìn	*v.* correspond	通信	3-4
同意	tóngyì	*v.* consent, approve, agree	同意	4-4
桶	tǒng	*n.* bin, bucket, barrel	桶	2-3
痛快	tòngkuài	*adj.* delighted; *adv.* joyfully, greatly satisfied	痛快	1-1
偷偷地	tōutōude	*adv.* stealthily, secretly	偷偷地	4-3
土司	tǔsī	*n.* toast [transliteration]	土司	2-2
团	tuán	*n.* group, organization	團	1-3
退	tuì	*v.* return (things)	退	3-2

Simplified	Pinyin	English	Traditional	Lesson
W 外向	wàixiàng	*adj.* extrovert	外向	1-2
完	wán	*v.* finish; *adj.* complete	完	2-3
网络	wǎngluò	*n.* internet	網絡	1-4
网页	wǎngyè	*n.* homepage	網頁	1-4
网友	wǎngyǒu	*n.* internet friend	網友	1-4
网址	wǎngzhǐ	*n.* website	網址	1-4
忘掉	wàngdiào	*v.* forget	忘掉	4-2
喂	wèi	*v.* feed; *int.* hello	喂	2-4
胃口	wèikǒu	*n.* appetite	胃口	3-4
温水游泳池	wēnshuǐ yóuyǒngchí	*n.* heated pool	溫水游泳池	2-4
闻	wén	*v.* smell	聞	4-2
文身	wénshēn	*v. & n.* tatoo	文身	4-3
文学家	wénxuéjiā	*n.* writer, person of letters	文學家	2-4
问好	wènhǎo	*v.* send one's regards, say hello	問好	4-4
问路	wènlù	*v.* ask for directions	問路	1-1
问题	wèntí	*n.* problem, question	問題	2-2
吴	Wú	*n.* a surname	吳	1-2
物	wù	*n.* object, thing	物	4-4

Simplified	Pinyin	English	Traditional	Lesson
X 吸毒	xīdú	*v.* do drugs	吸毒	4-2
吸烟	xīyān	*v.* smoke (cigarette)	吸煙	3-2
稀饭	xīfàn	*n.* rice gruel, porridge	稀飯	2-2
稀有	xīyǒu	*adj.* scarce, unusual	稀有	2-4
希望	xīwàng	*v.* hope	希望	2-1
习惯	xíguàn	*v.* get used to	習慣	2-1
吓坏了	xià huài le	*colloq.* be terribly scared	嚇壞了	4-4
吓……一跳	xià...yí tiào	*v.* startle (someone)	嚇……一跳	4-1
咸	xián	*adj.* salty	鹹	2-2
咸肉	xiánròu	*n.* bacon	鹹肉	2-2
箱	xiāng	*n.* box	箱	1-1
香	xiāng	*adj.* appetizing, fragrant, aromatic	香	2-2
香肠	xiāngcháng	*n.* sausage	香腸	2-3

Simplified	Pinyin	English	Traditional	Lesson
香烟	xiāngyān	*n.* cigarette	香煙	4-2
相信	xiāngxìn	*v.* believe	相信	2-4
向	xiàng	*prep.* towards or to; *v.* turn towards	向	1-1
项目	xiàngmù	*n.* item	項目	1-3
小菜	xiǎocài	*n.* 1. side dish; 2. relishes, pickles, ect.	小菜	2-2
小吃店	xiǎochīdiàn	*n.* small restaurant, snack bar	小吃店	2-3
小卖部	xiǎomàibù	*n.* tuck-shop, canteen	小賣部	3-3
小生	xiǎoshēng	*n.* young man (a role in Chinese opera)	小生	4-1
小题大做	xiǎotí-dàzuò	*idiom* make a mountain out of a molehill	小題大做	4-2
新潮	xīncháo	*n.* new trend; *adj.* trendy, fashionable	新潮	4-3
新鲜	xīnxiān	*adj.* fresh	新鮮	2-1
心里	xīnli	in (one's) heart	心裡	4-3
心目中	xīnmùzhōng	*phr.* in one's eyes	心目中	4-1
心情	xīnqíng	*n.* mood	心情	2-4
选	xuǎn	*v.* elect, choose	選	1-2
选择	xuǎnzé	*v.* choose; *n.* option, choice	選擇	1-3

Y 烟味	yānwèi	*n.* cigarette smell	煙味	3-2
颜色	yánsè	*n.* colour	顏色	3-3
养老院	yǎnglǎoyuàn	*n.* retirement village	養老院	4-1
要	yào	*v.* ask for; want	要	3-1
要好	yàohǎo	*adj.* good (friendship), close (friendship)	要好	3-4
野餐	yěcān	*n.* picnic	野餐	2-3
也好	yěhǎo	*phr.* may as well, may not be a bad idea	也好	3-2
页	yè	*n.* page	頁	4-1
叶	yè	*n.* foliage, leaf	葉	2-4
一旦	yídàn	*adv.* once, in case, now that	一旦	4-2
一切	yíqiè	*n.* everything, all	一切	2-1
一阵子	yízhènzi	*colloq.* a while, a short period of time	一陣子	2-4
一边… 一边…	yìbiān… yìbiān…	do one thing while doing another	一邊… 一邊…	2-3
一方面… 一方面…	yìfāngmiàn… yìfāngmiàn,,,	*conj.* for one thing..., for another...; on the one hand..., on the other hand...	一方面… 一方面…	2-1
一生	yìshēng	*adv.* throughout one's life	一生	2-4
一天到晚	yì tiān dào wǎn	*phr.* all day long, from morning till night	一天到晚	1-4
一直	yìzhí	*adv.* continuously; straight (in one direction)	一直	2-1
以后	yǐhòu	*adv.* after, later, afterwards	以後	2-3
意大利面	Yìdàlìmiàn	*n.* pasta (spaghetti, lasagne...)	義大利麵	2-2
印度	Yìndù	*n.* India	印度	2-2
拥吻	yōngwěn	*n.* hug and kiss	擁吻	3-1
永远	yǒngyuǎn	*adv.* forever	永遠	4-1
用功	yònggōng	*adj.* diligent, hard-working	用功	4-4
用心	yòngxīn	*adj.* attentive, diligent	用心	2-4
优美	yōuměi	*adj.* fine, exquisite	優美	2-1
邮件	yóujiàn	*n.* mail	郵件	1-4
油条	yóutiáo	*n.* deep-fried twisted dough stick	油條	2-2
游园会	yóuyuánhuì	*n.* fete	遊園會	1-2
犹豫	yóuyù	*v.* hesitate, be undecided	猶豫	3-3

Simplified	Pinyin	English	Traditional	Lesson
有的	yǒude	*adj.* some, a few	有的	2-3
有害	yǒuhài	*adj.* harmful	有害	4-2
有朋自远方来	yǒu péng zì yuǎnfāng lái	a friend from afar	有朋自遠方來	2-1
有趣	yǒuqù	*adj.* interesting, fun	有趣	1-3
有学问	yǒuxuéwèn	*adj.* knowledgeable	有學問	2-4
玉红	Yùhóng	*n.* a woman's name	玉紅	2-4
员工	yuángōng	*n.* employee	員工	3-2
远方	yuǎnfāng	*n.* distant place	遠方	2-1
乐器	yuèqì	*n.* musical instrument	樂器	1-2
运动会	yùndònghuì	*n.* sports carnival	運動會	1-2
运气	yùnqì	*n.* luck	運氣	3-2
Z 杂货店	záhuòdiàn	*n.* grocery store	雜貨店	3-2
载	zài	*v.* convey by vehicles, ships, etc.	載	2-3
在于	zài yú	*v.* be determined by, depend on	在於	4-2
赞成	zànchéng	*v.* approve of, agree with	贊成	4-1
脏	zāng	*adj.* dirty	臟	3-2
增加	zēngjiā	*v.* add, increase	增加	1-3
章	Zhāng	*n.* a surname; [zhāng] chapter	章	1-2
招	zhāo	*v.* recruit	招	3-1
照顾	zhàogù	*v.* take care of, look after	照顧	1-1, 2-4
着	zhe	*part.* used to indicate a continuing state, or an action in progress	著	1-1
真是的	zhēnshìde	*colloq.* used to remark on something unpleasant	真是的	1-4
挣	zhèng	*v.* earn, make (money)	掙	3-1
正在	zhèngzài	*adv.* in process of (indicates an action is in progress)	正在	1-3
纸箱	zhǐxiāng	*n.* carton	紙箱	2-3
制服	zhìfú	*n.* uniform	制服	3-1
重要	zhòngyào	*adj.* important	重要	4-4
祝福	zhùfú	*v.* offer good wishes	祝福	3-4
专心	zhuānxīn	*v.* concentrate; *adj.* attentive, asorbed	專心	2-4, 4-4
转圈	zhuànquān	*v.* go around in a circle, turn in a circle	轉圈	2-1
壮	zhuàng	*adj.* strong, muscular	壯	4-1
撞上	zhuàngshang	*v.* run into, strike	撞上	4-4
准	zhǔn	*v.* allow	准	4-2
资料	zīliào	*n.* data, information	資料	1-1, 1-4
自从	zìcóng	*prep.* since, ever since	自從	4-4
自相矛盾	zìxiāng-máodùn	*idiom* be self-contradictory	自相矛盾	4-3
走走	zǒuzou	*v.* travel around, walk around	走走	2-4
组	zǔ	*n.* group	組	1-3
作怪	zuòguài	*v.* act mischievously, create mischief	作怪	4-3

Appendix 2

WORDS AND EXPRESSIONS
English-Chinese

English	Simplified	Pinyin
A		
a while, a short period of time	一阵子	yízhènzi
absolutely, really *(colloq.)*	可……了	kě...le
absorbed, attentive	专心	zhuānxīn
achievement, result	成绩	chéngjī
activity	活动	huódòng
actually, the very end	究竟	jiūjìng
adapt, get used to	适应	shìyìng
add	加	jiā
add, increase	增加	zēngjiā
addicted to	上瘾	shàngyǐn
Adelaide	阿德莱德	Ādéláidé
adore, worship	崇拜	chóngbài
advertisement	广告	guǎnggào
afraid of	怕	pà
after, afterwards	以后	yǐhòu
after all, really	到底	dàodǐ
afterwards, then	然后	ránhòu
agree with	赞成	zànchéng
agree, approve	同意	tóngyì
air	空气	kōngqì
all day long, from morning till night	一天到晚	yì tiān dào wǎn
all you can eat	任你吃到饱	rèn nǐ chī dào bǎo
allegedly, it is said	据说	jùshuō
almost	几乎	jīhū
allow	准	zhǔn
also, in addition	而且	érqiě
always, all the time	老是	lǎoshì
and, with	跟	gēn
and so forth, and so on	等	děng
and so on *(colloq.)*	什么的	shénmede
annoying	气人	qìrén
another	另	lìng
any, whatever	任何	rènhé
anyway, anyhow	反正	fǎnzhèng
apart from	除了……以外	chúle...yǐwài
apologize	道歉	dàoqiàn
appetite	胃口	wèikǒu
appetizing, fragrant	香	xiāng
apply for	申请	shēnqǐng
apply, rub	擦	cā
approve of	赞成	zànchéng
area, district	区	qū
argument, truth	道理	dàoli
arrange	安排	ānpái
arrogant, conceited	骄傲	jiāo'ào
as a result, in the end	结果	jiéguǒ
as for...	对……来说	duì...lái shuō
ask for, want	要	yào
ask for directions	问路	wènlù
ask for sth. undesirable	惹	rě
at ease, stop worrying	放心	fàngxīn
at the time (when sth. happens)	临时	línshí
at that time, then	当时	dāngshí
attentive, absorbed	专心	zhuānxīn
attentive, diligent	用心	yòngxīn
attitude	态度	tàidù
awfully, terribly *(colloq.)*	不可开交	bù kě kāi jiāo
Ayers Rock	艾尔岩	Ài'ěryán
B		
baby-sitter	保姆	bǎomǔ
bacon	咸肉	xiánròu
bad thing, evil deed	坏事	huàishì
bake, roast, toast	烤	kǎo
bar, pub	酒馆	jiǔguǎn
barbecue	烤肉	kǎoròu
barbecue chicken	烤鸡	kǎojī
be, work as	当	dāng
beach, seashore	海边	hǎibiān
beauty salon	美容院	měiróngyuàn
become	成为	chéngwéi
beer	啤酒	píjiǔ
behave, behaviour	表现	biǎoxiàn
Beihai Park	北海公园	Běihǎi Gōngyuán
believe	相信	xiāngxìn
beneath, under	底下	dǐxia
besides	除了……以外	chúle...yǐwài
beyond one's imagination	不可思议	bù kě sīyì

English	Simplified	Pinyin	English	Simplified	Pinyin
big deal, serious	大不了	dàbuliǎo	class meeting	班会	bānhuì
bin, bucket, barrel	桶	tǒng	clearly, obviously	明明	míngmíng
black tea	红茶	hóngchá	clerk, salesperson	店员	diànyuán
blunderer, bungler	糊涂虫	hútuchóng	clever	聪明	cōngming
body	身体	shēntǐ	client, customer	顾客	gùkè
boot (of car)	车箱	chēxiāng	close (friendship)	要好	yàohǎo
boss	老板	lǎobǎn	coffee	咖啡	kāfēi
bottle, jar	瓶子	píngzi	coffee shop	咖啡馆	kāfēiguǎn
bottoms up	干杯	gānbēi	colour	颜色	yánsè
bow	弓	gōng	come over	过来	guòlái
bowling	保龄球	bǎolíngqiú	comfortable, cosy	舒适	shūshì
box	箱	xiāng	commit (fault, crime)	犯	fàn
break down (computer)	死机	sǐjī	commit a crime	犯罪	fànzuì
break up, part company	分手	fēnshǒu	complain	抱怨	bàoyuàn
brew (tea or coffee)	泡	pào	computer game	电子游戏	diànzǐ yóuxì
bright, clever	聪明	cōngming	concentrate	专心	zhuānxīn
broke up (colloq.)	吹了	chuī le	condemn, scold	骂	mà
bustling	热闹	rènào	Confucius	孔子	Kǒngzǐ
			congratulations	恭喜	gōngxǐ
C			conscientious, earnest	认真	rènzhēn
camp; camping	露营	lùyíng	consent, agree	同意	tóngyì
can, be capable of	能够	nénggòu	conservative	保守	bǎoshǒu
Canberra	堪培拉	Kānpéilā	consider that...	认为	rènwéi
candidate	人选	rénxuǎn	consume a lot of	耗电	hàodiàn
cannot endure/stand	受不了	shòubuliǎo	electricity		
canteen	小卖部	xiǎomàibù	contact, get in touch with	联系	liánxì
capable of, can	能够	nénggòu	continue	继续	jìxù
care about	关心	guānxīn	continuously	一直	yìzhí
carry (luggage)	提	tí	continuously, frequently	不停地	bù tíng de
carton	纸箱	zhǐxiāng	contradictory	矛盾	máodùn
catch up with, pursue	赶	gǎn	convenient	方便	fāngbiàn
CD Rom	光盘	guāngpán	convey (by vehicles)	载	zài
cereal	谷类食物	gǔ lèi shíwù	cool (slang)	酷	kù
change, exchange	换	huàn	correspond	通信	tōngxìn
charming	迷人	mírén	create disturbance,	闹事	nàoshì
chat	聊	liáo	make trouble		
chat	聊天儿	liáotiānr	create mischief	作怪	zuòguài
chat room	聊天室	liáotiān shì	curry	咖喱	gālí
chess	国际象棋	guójì xiàngqí	customer	顾客	gùkè
child	孩子	háizi	cut into a queue	插队	chāduì
Chinese couplet	对联	duìlián	**D**		
choir	合唱团	héchàngtuán	data, information	资料	zīliào
choose, choice	选择	xuǎnzé	day dream	白日梦	báirìmèng
choose, elect	选	xuǎn	decide	决定	juédìng
cigarette	香烟	xiāngyān	deep-fried twisted	油条	yóutiáo
cigarette smell	烟味	yānwèi	dough stick		
class leader	班长	bānzhǎng			

English	Simplified	Pinyin
delighted, joyfully	痛快	tòngkuài
depend on	在于	zài yú
deposit, save	存	cún
design	设计	shèjì
determined by, be -	在于	zài yú
die	死（掉）	sǐ (diào)
differ (by), be short	差	chà
dilemma, in a -; contradictory	矛盾	máodùn
diligent, attentive	用心	yòngxīn
diligent, hard-working	用功	yònggōng
dinner party, have -	聚餐	jùcān
dirty	脏	zāng
disadvantage	坏处	huàichù
discover	发现	fāxiàn
discuss; discussion	讨论	tǎolùn
distant place	远方	yuǎnfāng
disturb, interrupt	吵	chǎo
diverse and plentiful	丰富	fēngfù
do one thing while doing another	一边…… 一边……	yìbiān... yìbiān...
Don't you think it's annoying?	你说气不气人?	Nǐ shuō qì bú qìrén?
doze off	打瞌睡	dǎ kēshuì
drag, pull	扯	chě
drawback	坏处	huàichù
dress up, style of dress	打扮	dǎbàn
drink wine/liquor	喝酒	hē jiǔ
drugs, do -	吸毒	xīdú
dusk, early evening	傍晚	bàngwǎn
dye	染	rǎn

E

English	Simplified	Pinyin
e-mail	电子邮件	diànzǐ yóujiàn
e-mail address	电子邮址	diànzǐ yóuzhǐ
each other, mutually	互相	hùxiāng
elect, choose	选	xuǎn
earn	挣	zhèng
electricity	电	diàn
embarrassing, lose face (*colloq.*)	丢人	diūrén
employee	员工	yuángōng
empty	空	kōng
encounter	碰	pèng
enter	进入	jìnrù
enthusiastic	热心	rèxīn
entire body	全身	quánshēn

English	Simplified	Pinyin
entire country	全国	quánguó
environment	环境	huánjìng
eucalyptus tree	桉树	ānshù
ever, once, formerly	曾经	céngjīng
ever since, since	自从	zìcóng
every country	各国	gèguó
every place	各处	gèchù
everything, all	一切	yíqiè
everywhere	到处	dàochù
example sentence	例句	lìjù
except	除了……以外	chúle...yǐwài
exchange, swap	交换	jiāohuàn
exercise, practise	练习	liànxí
experience	经验	jīngyàn
expose to sunlight	晒	shài
express one's gratitude	道谢	dàoxiè
exquisite	优美	yōuměi
extremely (*colloq.*)	不得了	bùdéliǎo
extrovert	外向	wàixiàng

F

English	Simplified	Pinyin
facsimile	传真	chuánzhēn
famous brand	名牌	míngpái
famous, celebrated	鼎鼎大名	dǐngdǐng dàmíng
fashion shop	服饰店	fúshìdiàn
fashionable, trendy	新潮	xīncháo
fast-food restaurant	快餐店	kuàicāndiàn
fault, mistake	毛病	máobìng
fax machine	传真机	chuánzhēnjī
feed	喂	wèi
feel, feeling	感觉	gǎnjué
fete	游园会	yóuyuánhuì
fine, exquisite	优美	yōuměi
finish	完	wán
flower	花	huā
fluent	流利	liúlì
follow, accompany	跟	gēn
for one thing..., for another...	一方面…… 一方面……	yìfāngmiàn... yìfāngmiàn...
forbid, not allow	不准	bùzhǔn
forever	永远	yǒngyuǎn
forget	忘掉	wàngdiào
form teacher	班主任	bānzhǔrèn
fragrant, aromatic	香	xiāng
fresh	新鲜	xīnxiān
fried egg	煎蛋	jiāndàn
fried noodle	炒面	chǎomiàn

English	Simplified	Pinyin	English	Simplified	Pinyin
friend from afar	有朋自远方来		hesitate	犹豫	yóuyù
		yǒu péng zì yuǎnfāng lái	hide	藏	cáng
from morning till night	一天到晚	yì tiān dào wǎn	hold, operate	开	kāi
from, since	从	cóng	holiday	假期	jiàqī
fun, interesting	有趣	yǒuqù	homepage	网页	wǎngyè
function	功能	gōngnéng	hope	希望	xīwàng
future	将来	jiānglái	hospitable, warm	热情	rèqíng
			hot (of taste)	辣	là

G

			hot pot	火锅	huǒguō
garbage	垃圾	lājī	hotel	旅馆	lǚguǎn
get along well	谈得来	tán de lái	hug and kiss	拥吻	yōngwěn
get in touch with	联系	liánxì	husband	丈夫	zhàngfu
get on the internet	上网	shàng wǎng			

I

get used to	适应;	shìyìng;	idiom	成语	chéngyǔ
	习惯	xíguàn	important	重要	zhòngyào
get, receive (money, prize)	领	lǐng	in (one's) heart	心里	xīnli
give a farewell party	饯行	jiànxíng	in addition to	除了……以外	chúle...yǐwài
give a word, say (it)	说一声	shuō yì shēng	in fashion, popular	流行	liúxíng
go around in a circle	转圈	zhuànquān	in one's eyes	心目中	xīnmùzhōng
go past	经过	jīngguò	in process of	正在	zhèngzài
golf	高尔夫球	gāo'ěrfūqiú	in the class	班上	bānshàng
good (friendship)	要好	yàohǎo	in the spotlight	出风头	chūfēngtou
good, fine, beautiful	佳	jiā	increase	增加	zēngjiā
graduate	毕业	bìyè	India	印度	Yìndù
Great Barrier Reef	大堡礁	Dàbǎojiāo	inevitable	难免	nánmiǎn
grocery store	杂货店	záhuòdiàn	information, data	资料	zīliào
group	组	zǔ	intelligent, bright	聪明	cōngming
group, organization	团	tuán	interesting, fun	有趣	yǒuqù
guess [riddle]	打	dǎ	international	国际	guójì
guilty about, feel -	过意不去	guòyì búqù	internet	网络	wǎngluò
gymnastics	体操	tǐcāo	internet friend	网友	wǎngyǒu
			introvert	内向	nèixiàng

H

			it is said, allegedly	据说	jùshuō
hah	哈	hā	it's a pity, too bad	可惜	kěxī
handsome	帅;	shuài;	item	项目	xiàngmù
	英俊	yīngjùn			

J

happy, rejoice	开心	kāixīn	jar, jug, tin, can	罐子	guànzi
harmful	有害	yǒuhài	join in	加入	jiārù
have a holiday/vacation	放假	fàngjià	joyfully, greatly satisfied	痛快	tòngkuài
have mercy on	饶	ráo	junk, waste	废品	fèipǐn
having contradicting thoughts	矛盾	máodùn	just, only just	才	cái

K

heart set on (something or someone)	动心	dòngxīn	kangaroo	袋鼠	dàishǔ
heat	加温	jiāwēn	karate	空手道	kōngshǒudào
heated pool	温水游泳池		kebab	肉串	ròuchuàn
		wēnshuǐ yóuyǒngchí	king	国王	guówáng
help, helpful	帮忙	bāngmáng			

English	Simplified	Pinyin
know, recognize	认识	rènshi
knowledgeable	有学问	yǒuxuéwèn
koala (in China)	考拉	kǎolā
(in Taiwan)	无尾熊	wúwěixióng

L

English	Simplified	Pinyin
lamb stew	炖羊肉	dùnyángròu
later, after	以后	yǐhòu
lead the way	带路	dàilù
leaf, foliage	叶	yè
learn by heart	背	bèi
leave	离开	líkāi
left, remain	剩下	shèngxià
lettuce	生菜	shēngcài
liberal, open-minded	开通	kāitōng
lie	说谎	shuōhuǎng
local	地方	dìfāng
look after	照顾	zhàogù
lose	丢	diū
lose face	丢人	diūrén
lose temper	发脾气	fā píqi
lose weight	减肥	jiǎnféi
lost in thought	发呆	fādāi
luck	运气	yùnqì

M

English	Simplified	Pinyin
mail	邮件	yóujiàn
make a mountain out of a molehill	小题大做	xiǎotí-dàzuò
make friends	交朋友	jiāo péngyou
make money	挣钱	zhèng qián
make trouble	捣蛋	dǎodàn
make trouble, create disturbance	闹事	nàoshì
make use of	利用	lìyòng
material (fabric)	料子	liàozi
may as well, may not be a bad idea	也好	yěhǎo
meal	餐	cān
meet, pick up (someone)	接	jiē
m.w. (cigarette)	根	gēn
m.w. (glasses, couplet)	副	fù
meat pie	烤肉饼	kǎoròubǐng
memorize	背	bèi
mention	提	tí
messy	乱	luàn
mischievously, act -	作怪	zuòguài
mood	心情	xīnqíng

English	Simplified	Pinyin
most	大部分	dàbùfen
mostly	多半	duōbàn
Movie World	电影世界	Diànyǐng Shìjiè
muscular, strong	壮	zhuàng
music store	唱片行	chàngpiànháng
musical instrument	乐器	yuèqì
mutually, each other	互相	hùxiāng
my or our (humble form)	敝	bì

N

English	Simplified	Pinyin
nag	唠叨	láodāo
name	陈英	Chén Yīng
nanny	保姆	bǎomǔ
national	全国	quánguó
navel	肚脐	dùqí
navel piercing	肚脐洞	dùqídòng
new trend, trendy	新潮	xīncháo
new word	生词	shēngcí
newsboy	送报员	sòngbàoyuán
noisy	吵	chǎo
non-smoking area	非吸烟区	fēi xīyān qū
noodle soup	汤面	tāngmiàn
noodles	面条	miàntiáo
not allow, forbid	不准	bùzhǔn
(not) at all	并（不）	bìng(bù)
not only...but also	不但…… 而且……	búdàn...érqiě
nothing more, that's all	而已	éryǐ

O

English	Simplified	Pinyin
oatmeal porridge	麦片粥	màipiànzhōu
object, thing	物	wù
odd, strange, weird	怪怪的	guàiguàide
offer good wishes	祝福	zhùfú
old fogey	老古板	lǎogǔbǎn
on behalf of others	代	dài
on one's body	身上	shēnshàng
on the one hand..., on the other hand...	一方面…… 一方面……	yìfāngmiàn... yìfāngmiàn...
once, formerly, ever	曾经	céngjīng
once, in case, now that	一旦	yídàn
one after another	陆续	lùxù
open-minded	开通；开明	kāitōng; kāimíng
opera house	歌剧院	gējùyuàn
opinion, viewpoint	看法	kànfǎ
option	选择	xuǎnzé

English	Simplified	Pinyin
other people	别人	biérén
other, others	其他	qítā
overdose	过量	guòliàng
P		
page	页	yè
pair	副	fù
parents	父母亲	fùmǔqīn
part company, break up	分手	fēnshǒu
part-time job, have -	打工	dǎgōng
pass by	路过	lùguò
(passive signifier)	被	bèi
passive smoking	二手烟	èrshǒuyān
pasta (spaghetti, lasagne...)	意大利面	Yìdàlìmiàn
paste	贴	tiē
pay (bill, money)	付	fù
peculiar	特有	tèyǒu
pedestrian crossing	人行横道	rénxíng héngdào
perhaps, maybe	说不定	shuōbudìng
person of letters	文学家	wénxuéjiā
personality	个性	gèxìng
Perth	珀斯	Pòsī
pick up (someone)	接	jiē
picnic	野餐	yěcān
pierce, penetrate	穿	chuān
pizza	比萨饼	bǐsàbǐng
place, location	地方	dìfāng
plain steamed bun	馒头	mántou
plastic bag	塑料袋	sùliàodài
plate	盘子	pánzi
please have the best seat	请上坐	qǐng shàngzuò
pocket money	零花钱	línghuāqián
poke	刺	cì
poor, not up to standard	差	chà
popular (person)	出风头	chūfēngtou
popular, in fashion	流行	liúxíng
popularity	人缘儿	rényuánr
porridge, rice gruel	稀饭	xīfàn
practice	练习	liànxí
practise	练	liàn
prepare, arrange	筹备	chóubèi
price	价钱	jiàqián
prince charming	白马王子	báimǎ-wángzǐ
problem, question	问题	wèntí

English	Simplified	Pinyin
propose a toast	敬	jìng
protect, protection	保护	bǎohù
provoke	惹	rě
pub, bar	酒馆	jiǔguǎn
pull, drag	扯	chě
pursue, catch up with	赶	gǎn
put on, rub	擦	cā
Q		
quarrel	吵（架）	chǎo (jià)
question, problem	问题	wèntí
quit smoking	戒烟	jièyān
quit, give up	戒	jiè
quit, resign, sack	辞掉	cídiào
R		
raw vegetable	生菜	shēngcài
really	实在	shízài
really, on earth	到底	dàodǐ
receipt	收据	shōujù
receive, bear	受	shòu
receive (message)	接	jiē
receive (money, prize)	领	lǐng
recognize, know	认识	rènshi
recruit	招	zhāo
recycle	回收	huíshōu
red through and through	红通通	hóngtōngtōng
reference book	参考书	cānkǎoshū
rejoice, happy	开心	kāixīn
relation, relationship	关系	guānxì
relations with people	人缘儿	rényuánr
remain, be left	剩下	shèngxià
remark on something unpleasant	真是的	zhēnshìde
report	报告	bàogào
resign, sack, quit	辞掉	cídiào
respectively	各自	gèzì
restaurant	餐馆；餐厅	cānguǎn; cāntīng
result	结果	jiéguǒ
retirement village	养老院	yǎnglǎoyuàn
return (things)	退	tuì
return, reward	回报	huíbào
reward	回报	huíbào
rice gruel, porridge	稀饭	xīfàn
ring, hoop	环	huán
room	房间	fángjiān
row, rowing	划船	huáchuán

English	Simplified	Pinyin
rubbish, garbage	垃圾	lājī
rule, regulation	规定	guīdìng
run into, strike	撞上	zhuàngshang

S

English	Simplified	Pinyin
sad	难过	nánguò
salad	沙拉	shālā
salary, wage	工资	gōngzī
salesperson, clerk	店员	diànyuán
salty	咸	xián
sausage	香肠	xiāngcháng
save, deposit	存	cún
say (it), give a word	说一声	shuō yì shēng
say hello	问好	wènhǎo
scarce, unusual	稀有	xīyǒu
scenery	风景	fēngjǐng
scholarship	奖学金	jiǎngxuéjīn
school starts	开学	kāixué
scold, condemn	骂	mà
Sea World	海洋世界	Hǎiyáng Shìjiè
seafood	海鲜	hǎixiān
seashore, seaside	海边	hǎibiān
secretly, stealthily	偷偷地	tōutōude
self-contradictory	自相矛盾	zìxiāng-máodùn
send (email, fax)	发	fā
send one's regards	问好	wènhǎo
serious, big deal (colloq.)	大不了	dàbuliǎo
sesame seed flatcake	烧饼	shāobǐng
set up, arrange, place	摆	bǎi
shield	盾	dùn
side	边	biān
side dish; pickles	小菜	xiǎocài
simple meal	便餐	biàncān
since, ever since	自从	zìcóng
since, from	从	cóng
small restaurant	小吃店	xiǎochīdiàn
smell (v.)	闻	wén
smoke (cigarette)	吸（烟）; 抽（烟）	xī(yān); chōu(yān)
smoothly, successfully	顺利	shùnlì
snack bar	小吃店	xiǎochīdiàn
so you say	说是这么说	shuō shì zhème shuō
softball	垒球	lěiqiú
solar energy	太阳能	tàiyángnéng
some, a few	有的	yǒude
Song dynasty	宋代	Sòngdài
sound, voice	声音	shēngyīn

English	Simplified	Pinyin
soya milk	豆浆	dòujiāng
speak out honestly	老实说来	lǎoshí shuō lái
spear	矛	máo
special	特别	tèbié
spend	花	huā
spend pocket money	零花	línghuā
sports carnival	运动会	yùndònghuì
stall	摊位	tānwèi
stand (v.)	立; 站	lì; zhàn
stand (n.), stall	摊位	tānwèi
stare blankly	发呆	fādāi
start, open	开	kāi
startle (someone)	吓……一跳	xià...yí tiào
stealthily, secretly	偷偷地	tōutōude
still	仍然	réngrán
stipulate	规定	guīdìng
stop worrying, at ease	放心	fàngxīn
strange, odd, weird	怪怪的	guàiguàide
strong, muscular	壮	zhuàng
stupid	笨	bèn
style	式样	shìyàng
style of dress; dress up	打扮	dǎbàn
style, manner, panache	派头	pàitóu
successfully, smoothly	顺利	shùnlì
sugar	糖	táng
suggest	提议	tíyì
suit; suitable	适合	shìhé
sun	太阳	tàiyáng
sunglasses	太阳镜	tàiyángjìng
sunscreen	防晒霜	fángshàishuāng
surprise	惊讶	jīngyà

T

English	Simplified	Pinyin
take a walk	散步	sànbù
take care of	照顾	zhàogù
take turns	轮	lún
talk, speak	讲话	jiǎnghuà
tatoo	文身	wénshēn
temper	脾气	píqi
tempt, urge, push	怂恿	sǒngyǒng
terribly scared (colloq.)	吓坏了	xià huài le
terribly, awfully (colloq.)	不可开交	bù kě kāi jiāo
text	课文	kèwén
thank	道谢	dàoxiè
that's all	而已	éryǐ
The Analects of Confucius	《论语》	Lúnyǔ

English	Simplified	Pinyin
then, afterwards	然后	ránhòu
then, at that time	当时	dāngshí
thing, object	物	wù
think that...	认为	rènwéi
throughout one's life	一生	yìshēng
throw	丢	diū
throw away	丢掉	diūdiào
time flies	光阴似箭	guāngyīn sì jiàn
tin, can, jar, jug	罐子	guànzi
toast (*n.*)	土司	tǔsī
toast, bake, roast	烤	kǎo
towards, to	向	xiàng
towards, with	跟	gēn
travel around	走走	zǒuzou
tree, wood	木	mù
trendy, new trend	新潮	xīncháo
trouble, troublesome	麻烦	máfan
trunk (of car)	车箱	chēxiāng
truth, argument	道理	dàoli
try	试	shì
try on (clothes/shoes)	试穿	shìchuān
tuck-shop	小卖部	xiǎomàibù
turn in a circle	转圈	zhuànquān
turn one's head	回头	huítóu
turn over	翻	fān
two different matters	两回事	liǎng huí shì

U

English	Simplified	Pinyin
Uluru	艾尔岩	Ài'ěryán
unable to resist/endure	禁不起	jīnbuqǐ
unavoidable	难免	nánmiǎn
unbearable	受不了	shòu bu liǎo
unbelievable	不可思议	bù kě sīyì
under, beneath	底下	dǐxia
understand	了解	liǎojiě
uniform	制服	zhìfú
upper garment	上衣	shàngyī
urge, push, tempt	怂恿	sǒngyǒng
use, make use of	利用	lìyòng
usually	通常	tōngcháng

V

English	Simplified	Pinyin
vacation	假期	jiàqī
vegetable	蔬菜	shūcài
video game	电子游戏	diànzǐ yóuxì
viewpoint	看法	kànfǎ
voice, sound	声音	shēngyīn
volleyball	排球	páiqiú

English	Simplified	Pinyin
W		
wage, salary	工资	gōngzī
waiter, waitress	服务员	fúwùyuán
walk around	走走	zǒuzou
walkman	随身听	suíshēntīng
warm, hospitable	热情	rèqíng
waste, junk	废品	fèipǐn
waste, wasteful	浪费	làngfèi
way	方式	fāngshì
wear (hat, ring)	戴	dài
wear (clothes, shoes)	穿	chuān
website	网址	wǎngzhǐ
well-known, celebrated	鼎鼎大名	dǐngdǐng dàmíng
when in Rome, do as the Romans do	入乡随俗	rùxiāng suí sú
why on earth; whatever for	干吗	gànmá
wife	妻子	qīzi
willing to	肯	kěn
word, term	词	cí
work as, serve as	当	dāng
worry	担心	dānxīn
worth the cost	划算	huásuàn
writer, man of letters	文学家	wénxuéjiā
Y		
young man (in opera)	小生	xiǎoshēng
your (respectful form)	贵	guì

Answers to riddles on p. 88

1. 毛笔 (Chinese brush)

2. 帽子 (hat)

3. 谜语 (riddle)

4. 名字 (name)

Appendix 3

CHARACTERS LEARNT IN 你好 1–4

(Characters learnt in this book are displayed in purple)

Chinese	Pinyin	English
1 Stroke		
一	yī	one
2 Strokes		
二	èr	two
七	qī	seven
九	jiǔ	nine
了	le	(grammatical word)
十	shí	ten
八	bā	eight
人	rén	person, people; personality
儿	ér	(word ending); son
几	jǐ	how many; a few
又	yòu	again
3 Strokes		
三	sān	three
下	xià	latter part; under; next; to get off
才	cái	just, only just
久	jiǔ	long (length of time)
也	yě	also, too, as well
习	xí	to practise; to be used to
千	qiān	thousand
上	shàng	to go to, board; up, above, on; previous
个	gè	(measure word); individual
么	me	(word ending)
工	gōng	work, job
大	dà	big, large
小	xiǎo	little, small
口	kǒu	mouth
山	shān	mountain
门	mén	door, gate
己	jǐ	oneself
已	yǐ	already
子	zi; zǐ	[suffix]; son
女	nǚ	woman, female, daughter, girl
飞	fēi	to fly
马	mǎ	horse

Chinese	Pinyin	English
4 Strokes		
五	wǔ	five
开	kāi	to open; to drive; to start; to operate; away
不	bù	no, not
中	zhōng	centre, middle; China
为	wèi; wéi	for; become, be
书	shū	book
午	wǔ	noon
历	lì	process
公	gōng	public; metric
分	fēn	minute; cent; score; to part
什	shén	what
从	cóng	from, since
以	yǐ	to use
今	jīn	present; today
六	liù	six
认	rèn	to recognize
队	duì	team, queue
友	yǒu	friend
太	tài	too
天	tiān	day; sky
少	shǎo	few, little
车	chē	vehicle
牙	yá	tooth
日	rì	day; sun
水	shuǐ	water
见	jiàn	to see
手	shǒu	hand
牛	niú	ox, cow
毛	máo	10 cent unit; body hair, fur
气	qì	manner, air; to annoy, to be angry
长	cháng	long
	zhǎng	to grow; leader, chief
片	piàn; piān	thin piece or slice; film
父	fù	father
月	yuè	moon; month
风	fēng	wind
方	fāng	method; place
火	huǒ	fire

Chinese	Pinyin	English
心	xīn	heart

5 Strokes

Chinese	Pinyin	English
本	běn	(m.w. for books etc.); original
东	dōng	east
平	píng	flat, level, ordinary
且	qiě	also, moreover
电	diàn	electricity
史	shǐ	history
乐	yuè; lè	music; happy
半	bàn	half
用	yòng	to use
他	tā	he, him; other
们	men	(plural word)
包	bāo	to wrap; bag
北	běi	north
写	xiě	to write
让	ràng	let, to allow
出	chū	to go/come out
加	jiā	to add, to increase
台	tái	broadcasting station; (m.w. for TV)
对	duì	correct; opposite; pair
发	fā; fà	to happen, to send; hair
去	qù	to go; last (year)
左	zuǒ	left
功	gōng	merit; effort
节	jié	section; festival
头	tóu	head
只	zhī; zhǐ	(m.w. for animals); only
右	yòu	right
可	kě	may
号	hào	date; number
叫	jiào	to be called, to call
叨	dāo	talkative
四	sì	four
外	wài	outside
冬	dōng	winter
处	chù	place, point, part
边	biān	(word ending - location); side
术	shù	technique, art
正	zhèng	just, straight, exactly
旧	jiù	old, worn
汉	hàn	name of a Chinese dynasty
打	dǎ	to hit, to play (tennis...etc.), to dial, to guess (riddle)
母	mǔ	mother
业	yè	business; course of study

Chinese	Pinyin	English
目	mù	item; eye
生	shēng	to be born, to get; raw; unfamiliar; student
白	bái	white

6 Strokes

Chinese	Pinyin	English
再	zài	again
亚	yà	second
年	nián	year
买	mǎi	to buy
后	hòu	behind, after; queen
同	tóng	same; together
网	wǎng	net
共	gòng	together
关	guān	to concern; to close; to relate
兴	xìng	pleasure
件	jiàn	(m.w. for mail, clothes...)
份	fèn	(m.w. for job, report...)
休	xiū	to stop, to rest
任	rèn	to allow, to let; official post
会	huì	to be able to; be likely to; meeting
先	xiān	first, in advance
交	jiāo	to cross, to interact
决	jué	to decide
次	cì	(m.w. for times)
那	nà	that
刚	gāng	just now, just
动	dòng	to move
欢	huān	happy
地	dì	floor, earth, ground, place
	de	grammtical word
在	zài	(in progress); at, on, in
当	dāng	to be, to serve as; at the time
吗	ma	(question word)
吃	chī	to eat
吐	tù; tǔ	to vomit; to spit
吸	xī	to inhale
向	xiàng	towards, to; to turn towards; direction
回	huí	to return; to turn around; (m.w. for matters)
因	yīn	cause
岁	suì	year of age
师	shī	teacher
行	xíng	to walk, to travel; O.K.
	háng	business firm
多	duō	many, much, more; how (e.g. long)

Chinese	Pinyin	English
名	míng	name; famous
各	gè	every, each
问	wèn	to ask
字	zì	character, word
过	guò	to pass, cross
好	hǎo	good, fine
她	tā	she, her
妈	mā	mother
如	rú	if
红	hóng	red
级	jí	grade, level
机	jī	aircraft, machine; opportunity
成	chéng	to become, to succeed
收	shōu	to collect
早	zǎo	early; morning
有	yǒu	to have, there is/are
灯	dēng	light
忙	máng	busy
百	bǎi	hundred
老	lǎo	old (living things); elderly; always
考	kǎo	to take or give a test/exam
西	xī	west
而	ér	yet
页	yè	page
肉	ròu	meat
自	zì	self, since
衣	yī	clothes
米	mǐ	rice

7 Strokes

Chinese	Pinyin	English
两	liǎng	two
来	lái	to come
更	gèng	even, more
医	yī	doctor, medicine
弟	dì	younger brother
你	nǐ	you
住	zhù	to live
作	zuò	to do
但	dàn	but, however
低	dī	low
体	tǐ	body
冷	lěng	cold
邮	yóu	mail
别	bié	distinction; don't; other
块	kuài	dollar; (m.w. for dollar); piece
坏	huài	bad, to go bad
址	zhǐ	location, site

Chinese	Pinyin	English
坐	zuò	to sit; to take (a bus, train, etc.)
花	huā	to spend; flower
寿	shòu	longevity
听	tīng	to hear, to listen
吧	ba	(suggestion word)
吹	chuī	to blow
吵	chǎo	noisy; to quarrel, to disturb
园	yuán	garden
希	xī	to hope
条	tiáo	strip; (m.w. for long and thin object)
饭	fàn	cooked rice, meal
饮	yǐn	to drink
应	yīng	should
	yìng	to adapt
间	jiān	within (a definite time or space); room; (m.w. for room)
这	zhè	this
还	hái; huán	also, still; to return (things)
进	jìn	to enter
运	yùn	to transport; luck
远	yuǎn	far
近	jìn	near, close
张	zhāng	(m.w. for paper); a surname; to stretch open
李	lǐ; Lǐ	plum; a surname
我	wǒ	I, me
时	shí	hour; time
没	méi	(negative word)
汽	qì	steam, vapour
找	zhǎo	to look for; to give change
把	bǎ	[grammatical word]
报	bào	to report; newspaper
肚	dù	abdomen
忘	wàng	to forget
快	kuài	happy; fast; soon
每	měi	every, each
男	nán	man, male
纸	zhǐ	paper
利	lì	sharp; smoothly; to benefit
走	zǒu	to go, to leave, to walk
里	lǐ	inside; unit of length
足	zú	foot
身	shēn	body

8 Strokes

Chinese	Pinyin	English
事	shì	business, matter, affair
果	guǒ	fruit, result

Chinese	Pinyin	English
卖	mài	to sell
直	zhí	continuously; straight
厕	cè	toilet
单	dān	single; list
其	qí	that, such
京	jīng	capital
话	huà	speech
该	gāi	should
试	shì	test; to try
参	cān	to participate
英	yīng	brave, elite
奇	qí	unusual, strange
呢	ne	(question word)
国	guó	nation, country
岸	àn	coast, shore
往	wàng	toward, to
备	bèi	to prepare
饱	bǎo	full
店	diàn	shop, store
空	kòng; kōng	free time; empty, sky
宜	yí	suitable
宠	chǒng	to spoil
定	dìng	to decide; certain
实	shí	truth
学	xué	to study, to learn
姓	xìng	family name, surname
姐	jiě	elder sister
妹	mèi	younger sister
始	shǐ	to start, to begin
经	jīng	to go through
练	liàn	to practise
玩	wán	to play, to have fun
现	xiàn	present
环	huán	to surround; ring, hoop
板	bǎn	board
狗	gǒu	dog
或	huò	or
些	xiē	[measure word] some; a little
明	míng	bright; tomorrow; to understand
易	yì	easy
泻	xiè	to have diarrhoea
泳	yǒng	swim
泡	pào	to brew (coffee/tea), to soak
抽	chōu	to smoke; to take out, to draw
物	wù	object, thing
受	shòu	to receive; to bear
爸	bà	father

Chinese	Pinyin	English
服	fú	clothes; to take (medicine); to serve
朋	péng	friend
放	fàng	to put, to let go, to let out
所	suǒ	so, place
性	xìng	character, nature
怪	guài	odd, strange
态	tài	attitude
视	shì	sight; to look at
金	jīn	gold
知	zhī	to know
和	hé	and, with
种	zhǒng	kind, type, sort
的	de	(possesive particle)
到	dào	to go to; to arrive; to
刮	guā	to blow (wind)
雨	yǔ	rain
非	fēi	not, wrong

9 Strokes

Chinese	Pinyin	English
南	nán	south
点	diǎn	hour; dot; a little
前	qián	front; before
便	pián	cheap
	biàn	urine or excrement; convenient
信	xìn	letter (mail); to believe
亲	qīng	related by blood
说	shuō	to speak, to say, to tell
语	yǔ	language
除	chú	except, besides; to divide (Maths)
茶	chá	tea
药	yào	medicine
封	fēng	(m.w. for letter); envelop
哪	nǎ	which, where
虽	suī	although
帮	bāng	to help, to assist
带	dài	to take, to bring; belt, tape
很	hěn	very
饼	bǐng	biscuit, cake, cookie
饺	jiǎo	dumpling (gold ingot-shaped)
度	dù	degree; to pass (time)
穿	chuān	to wear; to pierce
客	kè	guest; polite
室	shì	room
送	sòng	to escort; to give as present; to deliver
迷	mí	fan; to lose one's way; to charm

Chinese	Pinyin	English
选	xuǎn	to choose, to elect; choice
给	gěi	to give
结	jié	to conclude
相	xiàng	appearance, photograph
	xiāng	mutual, each other
架	jià	shelf, rack; (m.w. for fight)
轻	qīng	light (in weight)
比	bǐ	to compare; as...as
是	shì	is, am, are
昨	zuó	yesterday
星	xīng	star
春	chūn	spring
冒	mào	to risk, to emit
贵	guì	expensive; a respectful form of your
活	huó	to live; alive
觉	jué; jiào	to feel; sleep
拾	shí	to pick up; ten (e.g. written on cheque)
挣	zhèng	to earn, to make (money)
挺	tǐng	quite
看	kàn	to look at, see, watch, read
胖	pàng	fat, plump
怎	zěn	how
祝	zhù	to wish
科	kē	science
秋	qiū	autumn
要	yào	to want; to be going to; to ask for
差	chā	difference
	chà	be short of; poor (quality)
美	měi	beautiful
面	miàn	(word ending - location); noodle; aspect
香	xiāng	appetising; fragrant, aromatic
音	yīn	sound

10 Strokes

Chinese	Pinyin	English
哥	gē	elder brother
真	zhēn	really, truly; real, true
候	hòu	time
高	gāo	high, tall; height; a surname
离	lí	away from
凉	liáng	cool
准	zhǔn	to allow; standard; accurate
课	kè	lesson, subject
请	qǐng	please; to invite
谁	shéi	who, whom
谈	tán	to talk

Chinese	Pinyin	English
都	dōu	all; even
剧	jù	play, drama
能	néng	to be able to; ability; energy
难	nán	difficult
唠	láo	talkative
夏	xià	summer
饿	è	hungry
家	jiā	home, family; (as a suffix) designating the specialty of a person
害	hài	harm
容	róng	to hold; appearance
通	tōng	through; to get through
逛	guàng	to stroll
班	bān	class; duty
校	xiào	school
样	yàng	appearance
较	jiào	to compare; relatively
海	hǎi	sea
酒	jiǔ	wine, liquor
消	xiāo	to vanish
流	liú	to flow
拿	ná	to take, to bring (by hand)
换	huàn	to exchange, to change
特	tè	special
爱	ài	to love; love
脑	nǎo	brain
旅	lǚ	to travel
热	rè	hot
烤	kǎo	to roast, to bake, to toast, to grill
烟	yān	cigarette, smoke (*n.*)
息	xī	to rest; news
钱	qián	money
疼	téng	ache
病	bìng	sick, illness
站	zhàn	to stand; station, stop (*n.*)
顾	gù	to attend to
笑	xiào	to smile, to laugh; smile, laugh
被	bèi	a passive signifier
起	qǐ	to rise

11 Strokes

Chinese	Pinyin	English
假	jià	leave of absence; holiday
做	zuò	to do
停	tíng	to stop
象	xiàng	alike, resemble; elephant
菜	cài	dish, vegetable

Chinese	Pinyin	English
常	cháng	often, usual
唱	chàng	to sing
得	de; dé; děi	(degree, result of); to get; must
馆	guǎn	shop, building
骑	qí	to ride (on animal or bicycle)
绿	lù	green
绩	jī	result
理	lǐ	texture, reason, logic
球	qiú	ball
望	wàng	to expect
教	jiào; jiāo	to teach
晚	wǎn	late; evening, night
排	pái	row; to line up
接	jiē	to receive (message); to pick up (sb.) to answer (telephone)
您	nín	you (polite form)
惜	xī	to have pity on
惯	guàn	to get used to
累	lèi	tired
聊	liáo	to chat
票	piào	ticket
第	dì	(order)
着	zhe	a grammatical word
黄	huáng	yellow

12 Strokes

Chinese	Pinyin	English
舒	shū	comfortable
就	jiù	merely; at once
谢	xiè	to thank
喜	xǐ	to like; happy; happiness
喝	hē	to drink
街	jiē	street
牌	pái	brand; plate, sign
道	dào	way, raod; to say
暑	shǔ	heat, hot weather
最	zuì	the most
普	pǔ	general, universal
港	gǎng	port
渴	kě	thirsty
游	yóu	to swim; to play
期	qī	period
然	rán	like that

Chinese	Pinyin	English
愉	yú	happy, pleased
短	duǎn	short (length)
等	děng	to wait; and so on, etcetera
黑	hēi	black

13 Strokes

Chinese	Pinyin	English
楼	lóu	multi-storied building; storey, floor
数	shù; shǔ	numbers; to count
照	zhào	photograph; to tak (photograph); to take care of
新	xīn	new
感	gǎn	to feel; sense
想	xiǎng	to think
错	cuò	wrong
矮	ǎi	short, low (height)
简	jiǎn	simple
路	lù	road
跟	gēn	towards; with; and; to follow or accompany
零	líng	zero; small amount, fractions

14 Strokes

Chinese	Pinyin	English
境	jìng	area, place
赛	sài	to match, contest
歌	gē	song
慢	màn	slow
瘦	shòu	thin, lean; tight (fitting)
算	suàn	to calculate
粽	zòng	dumpling (in bamboo leaves)

15 Strokes

Chinese	Pinyin	English
影	yǐng	movie, shadow, image
澳	ào	bay
题	tí	topic; question

16 Strokes

Chinese	Pinyin	English
餐	cān	meal
赞	zàn	to support
篮	lán	basket
糕	gāo	cake, pudding